THE BALD TRILOGY
Furtive Nudist, Pigspurt, Jamais Vu

Furtive Nudist: 'It has a compelling fascination, as if one were being buttonholed for two and a half hours by a mixture of Ken Dodd and the Ancient Mariner.'   Michael Billington, *Guardian*

'Campbell has created a hilarious, mystifying, compelling one-man digest of all that lurks in the undercurrents when one swims out of the mainstream.'   Ian Shuttleworth, *Independent*

'The legendary Ken Campbell delivers a comic tour de force dredged from the folk memory of the Ilford basin.'   *Time Out*

Pigspurt: 'Three cheers for Ken Campbell's *Pigspurt* in which the erstwhile furtive nudist free-associates his way through nursery school and rep memories, an obsession with noses, Ken Dodd, faith healing and other random mental debris which finally coalesce in a burst of pink light and a sense that the riddle of the universe has been solved. There is nobody else like him.'   Irving Wardle, *Independent on Sunday*

'The only time I feel like dusting down the term "genius", in the pure sense of an influential demonic character, is when I'm confronted by a great Campbell show.'   Michael Coveney, *Observer*

Jamais Vu: 'Where does comic genius end and certified lunacy begin? . . . Your comic education isn't really complete until you have heard Campbell discoursing in pidgin English, and his account of life in the Republic of Vanuatu resembles the *National Geographic* magazine on mescaline . . . He achieves more moments of inspiration in a single show than most comedians manage in a lifetime and, once you have seen the world through his crazed eyes, it never looks quite the same again.'   Charles Spencer, *Daily Telegraph*

'Perhaps I am influenced by Campbell's bribe [socks], which festoon my feet as I write; but I don't think there is a more hilariously anarchic talent on the loose in the British theatre.'   Benedict Nightingale, *The Times*

'It is no accident he went to school in Barking. His contribution to British theatre is radical and immense.'   Andrew St George, *Financial Times*

Jamais Vu won the *Evening Standard* Best Comedy Award in 1993 and was nominated for two Olivier Awards in 1994.

Ken Campbell founded the Science Fiction Theatre of Liverpool in 1976 where he directed two monumental epics: the twenty-two hour cult show *The Warp*, and *Illuminatus!* which was chosen to open the Cottesloe at the National Theatre in London. He also founded the legendary *Ken Campbell's Roadshow*. He is the author of the children's plays *Old King Cole, Skungpoomery, School for Clowns, Clowns on a School Outing, Peef* and *Frank 'n' Stein*, plus books for two musicals: *Bendigo* and *Walking Like Geoffrey*. His film scripts have included *Unfair Exchanges*, which starred Julie Walters, and *The Madness Museum*. On television he played Fred Johnson, Alf Garnett's neighbour in *In Sickness and in Health*. Ken Campbell's three semi-autobiographical shows, *Furtive Nudist, Pigspurt* and *Jamais Vu*, were performed at the Royal National Theatre as *The Bald Trilogy* in 1993.

Ken Campbell

THE BALD TRILOGY

The Recollections of a Furtive Nudist

Pigspurt
– or Six Pigs from Happiness

Jamais Vu

with drawings by Eve Stewart

Methuen Drama

First published in Great Britain 1995
by Methuen Drama
an imprint of Reed Books Ltd
Michelin House, 81 Fulham Road, London SW3 6RB
and Auckland, Melbourne, Singapore and Toronto
and distributed in the United States of America by
Heinemann, a division of Reed Elsevier Inc.,
361 Hanover Street, Portsmouth, New Hampshire NH 03801 3959

A CIP catalogue record for this book
is available at the British Library
ISBN 0 413 69080 6

Thanks to Martin Fitzpatrick for his help with
the flick pictures

Typeset by Falcon, Wallington
Printed in Great Britain by
Clays Ltd, St Ives plc

Contents

The Recollections of a
Furtive Nudist

The voice had spoken to me, reminding me of
the place to which Horselover Fat had gone.
In his search . . . As we had been told, originally,
long ago, to do; I kept my commission.

Philip K. Dick
Valis

The Recollections of a Furtive Nudist
was directed by Gillian Brown at the Offstage
Downstairs, Camden Town, 21 June 1988.
Performed as an oral work by Ken Campbell
from 1988 to 1991 in England – Scotland – Wales –
Eire – Newfoundland – New York – Chicago – Amsterdam

Produced by Colin Watkeys

ONE

I was born in the War —
in London —
(Ilford actually) —
(Actually I was *conceived* as a result of the War —
my parents had long wanted a child —
but nothing was happening for them on that front —
then one night a low-flying doodle-bug over Ilford *whoooshes*
   the relevant juices into my formation) —
My earliest memories are of being under the dining-room
   table —
with my Mum —
(the table had a sheet of heavy metal on top of it) —
sometimes my Dad joining us —
and after the banging and the whizzing —
the silence —
only the sound of your own ears —
and then the 'All Clear' siren —
and I'm put into the toilet —
'To perform', they say —
And I think I may have given my best performances in there.

I used to perform for the creatures I fancied I could see in the
   lino —
old orange lino with that multi-coloured abstract patterning —

but I could divine swamps and jungles —
and the creatures —
very particularly the FROG —
bulging eyes —
no lips —
insistent, demanding smile —
it's the Frog who draws from me these extraordinary
    performances —
and not just performances —
sensational plotlines —
('Flying Bomb Riders of Africa', 'Christmas with the Red
    Indians') —
Also the Frog sometimes emanated a form of Knowledge —
encoded in rhythmic reiteration:
'In Ma a Roonoo-ko —
In Ma a Roonoo-ko —
In Ma a Roonoo-ko' —
and often delivered so forcefully it could still be received under
    the table —
some distance from the bathroom —
'In Ma a Roonoo-ko' —
Sometimes it was comforting to know that —
on other occasions just a little alarming.

Something else —
I had a partner —
As I recall it —
TWO OF US SAT THERE.

In his novel *Valis* the American author Philip K. Dick writes
    about his *alter ego* —

and he calls this *alter ego* 'Horselover Fat' —
A recent Philip K. Dick Society Newsletter reminds us how he
   came up with that name —
'Philip' in the Greek means 'admirer of the equestrian arts' —
and 'Dick' is the German for 'fat' —
HORSELOVER FAT —
If I do that with my name:
'Kenneth' in the Celtic means 'the handsome one' —
'Camp'? —
'Bell'? —
PRETTYBOY TENTRINGER —
So that's how I'll refer to my colleague of the lost toilet dramas:
Prettyboy Tentringer.

When I was eight (the war now well over) I was allowed to join
   the State Barkingside Saturday Morning Pictures Club —
There was a theory that if you could pitch an ice-cream tub just
   right you could get it to slide down the projector beam and hit
   the screen —
But only John Spooner had ever done it —
Waves of mass attempts to emulate John Spooner's feat would
   punctuate the proceedings —
One Saturday John Spooner got us all to bring a jam-jar of foul
   concoction of our own devising in to the cinema and take
   them (hidden under our jerseys) up into the circle —
During the Tex Ritter feature we all made hideous puke noises and
   emptied the jars onto the stalls.

Sadly John Spooner was to be very badly injured —
He'd brought along a box of matches and under the cinema
   seats was holding the Set Light to Your Farts Olympics —

and he set light to his trousers —
and had to have his arsehole grafted with a bit of his elbow.

— ? —

Soon as we're turned out of the State, a regular bunch of us mob
    up the road to the Fairlop Aerodrome —
this is a disused military airfield with swampy, stinky
    underground tunnels —
old gun turret bunker things called pillboxes —
and one Saturday word goes round that there's a German in one
    of the pillboxes —
we know our duty —
we go to rout him out —
dozen or so kids —
and there he is in the pillbox —
a little weaselly man and he's protecting some pages he's been
    writing —
and we chase him out —
we chase him right off the airfield —
and then we go back to that pillbox —
examine his pages —
and yes they are written in foreign —
and we pee on them —
we have a good group wee on them —
(which was all done quite decently: first of all us eight lads do
    our business on them and then the girls are sent in).

— ? —

But something about that —
the next week I return to the pillbox —
alone —
the German's not been back —

his yellowing pages —
I turn them over —
with a stick —
(the link between Germans and germs was well known at that
    time) —
and amongst the writing I find his drawings —
really terrific drawings —
of Red Indians —
there was 'Winnetou' the Red Indian Chief, and the young
    brave, 'Appanatshka' and —
(this one lovingly detailed) —
the beautiful Red Indian Squaw Princess 'NSCHO-TCHI'.

— ? —

From the bit I've had to do with the bringing up of my daughter
    I can confirm this:
young kids produce 'sticky' naturally —
they haven't necessarily been playing in the jam —
at times of excitement they just produce the stuff —
exude it —
this sticky —
and when I decided (at that moment of the decision) to take
    home the picture of Nscho-Tchi —
I exuded a load of it —
A record amount.

— ? —

But I was aware of twin health hazards here:
1. It was a German's —
2. It had been peed on —
and the portrait of Nscho-Tchi was not to survive its long soak in
    scalding Pine and Harpic water —

(except in memory —
I can recall it clearly to this day —
in all its detail).

— ❷ —

When I was 25 the phone rang —
It was my father —
he'd now retired —
he and my stepmother (my mother died when I was 12) had
    gone to live in Croyde, North Devon —
he wanted to know if I was ever going to visit them —
? —
'Yes', I said, 'I'll come now'.

— ❷ —

A35 van I had then —
and rounding the coastal bends, almost at Croyde, on the left,
    Saunton Sands —
a dunescape —
one is minded of the Moon —
I parked the van and set off over the Moon —
It was peculiarly hot that day —
(it was early Feb.) —
I returned to the van —
I hadn't thought to bring my trunks —
but I was stripping off —
down to my underpants —
(even right back in those days I always wore the 'boxer' style of
    underpant —
it was due to an article I'd read) —
and thus un-attired I was back over the dunes —

and the dunes and I were one —
and then I was addressed by a disembodied voice.

— ? —

And the Voice said: 'Why've you got your underpants on?' —
I said: 'Well . . . for decency' —
and the Voice said: 'But there's nobody about' —
? —
and I said: 'Yes, well, for sure we can't see anybody but
    somebody might pop up at any moment' —
'No', said the Voice, 'You've got your underpants on because
    you're scared to take them off.'

— ? —

Scared? —
Really? —
I wasn't scared of being arrested —
winding up in the Police Station —
I rather felt the tale you could tell afterwards would make it
    worth it —
so —
it was Dad —
I was very fond of that bloke —
and to be arrested for an antic like this just round the corner
    from where he'd just moved to —
No.

— ? —

So —
What I did —
I took down my underpants literally CIRCUMSPECTLY —

making sure, round 360 degrees, that I was unobserved —
and then I buried the pants under a bush —
and I took pains to MEMORIZE THAT BUSH —
and then I set off.

— 📍 —

Did you ever see Kurosawa's classic movie *Seven Samurai*? —
Remember how they run in it? —
Not like joggers —
they run knees bent and arse low —
(well they want to keep their bollocks out of the way of the
    arrows) —
and that's how I was —
low bush to little grass clump to low bush —
and suddenly overhead the ENEMY! —
THE AIR-SEA RESCUE HELICOPTER! —
I drop where I am —
cover my crime with sand —
but it occurs to me:
those guys are going to think something's up if they see me in
    the middle of this desolate duneworld building sandcastles —
they're going to think I'm an idiot in need of rescuing —
so I posed as a boffin almost at the conclusion of some algebraic
    conundrum I was working out in the sand —
'Unified field theory! —
Almost there —
if you'd just fuck off!' —
and they pass overhead —
and on.

— 📍 —

And up again and on —
in fits and spurts —

the Samurai —
aware round 360 degrees —
high sandbank to bush to clump —
and now I've come to the end of the Dunes and I'm faced with
    the challenge of the Great Plain.

— ❓ —

Wide open space now —
no cover —
a Canyon —
and I'm crouched behind the last bush and I feel great and I'll
    tell you who I am, I am Winnetou in his prime and it's not a
    question of WHETHER I'm going to take on the Challenge
    of the Canyon it's just a question of WHEN and the answer to
    When is when the juices are UP and the juices are UP and
    I'm over the Canyon and listen I have recall of FLYING over
    some parts of that terrain and I get a flash of who's going to
    be over there when I get there:
NSCHO-TCHI —
Nscho-Tchi is in them woods!

— ❓ —

But Nscho-Tchi had gone —
(there were signs she'd been there) —
it was getting cold —
I decided to go back.

— ❓ —

Re-traversing the Great Plain I just strolled —
it seemed to me it was now mine, this territory —

and that's when I was seen —
way up aloft, a man walking his dog, he saw me —
and I just turned fully to him and waved.

— ❓ —

And then back on the dunes —
and I thought 'Yeah that was a bright thing to do' (now
    samuraiing low) 'he's going to race round with that big dog
    and make a citizen's arrest' —
but clump, bush, dune and I've samuraied myself back to the
    well-remembered bush and pants now back on —
Wheee —
back in the van —
wheee —
Very nice my Dad's new place.

— ❓ —

And that night at my Dad's I had a dream —
(in certain company I have referred to it as a vision) —
anyway, in this dream, I understood Everything —
What we're all doing here —
The Grand Purpose, the Whole Show —
What we're meant to do —
What I was meant to do —
I thought, Fuck this is important —
so I woke myself up.

— ❓ —

And by the bedside was a book of crank speculation by a couple
    of Frenchmen —

(A couple of Frogs!) —
Louis Pauwels' and Jacques Bergier's *The Dawn of Magic* —
And I wrote on to the page it was opened at (page 98), all it
    seemed to me that would be necessary to reconjure the vision.

— ⑦ —

Next morning I read what I'd written:
'ENORMOUS SWIMMING BATH
VEGETATION AND FOLIAGE IN IT'

— ⑦ —

It wasn't enough! —
Why had I made no mention of the GEEZER? —
Yes that was the location, enormous swim bath of vegetation,
    but there'd been this geezer down there, the all-important
    geezer, and it was from him, presumably, I'd learnt . . .
what I'd now utterly forgotten —
And the more I tried to recall him —
the more it seemed that the act of recollection itself was driving
    him into the mists —
and Fog.

— ⑦ —

It was a couple of days later (still in Croyde) that a relative of
    my stepmother comes to stay —
and I'd not met him before —
and he was a great old soldier —
he'd been in Yalta in 1945 with Churchill, Roosevelt and
    Stalin —

he'd drunk Stalin under the table —
and it was very late now, there was just him and me up —
and he was telling me the most appalling military secrets —
and we got through a whole bottle of whisky —
EACH —
(Let me warn you about that last inch and a half of a bottle of
    whisky —
if it's not you who's doing the talking —
I think it might be damn near fatal) —
I was able to get out of the room with dignity —
but once I was in the corridor I knew it was medically advisable
    to CRAWL —
And I crawled to my room on the ground floor —
and I lay on the bed and the ceiling was swinging into the
    wall —
and I knew I'd done it this time —
this was permanent! —
And then I heard from the Voice.

— ❓ —

And the Voice said: 'Well you know what to do!' —
And I said: 'What NOW!?' —
(it was about half past two in the morning) —
and I'm looking out of the window and it does seem that
    everyone else is asleep —
certainly their lights are all out —
there's just the square of light on the lawn coming from my
    room.

— ❓ —

So —
I took all my clothes off —

and hopped out through the window —
and I skirt the square of light —
and I edge along the hedge —
and then I think I may have left my body for a few moments
    because I have vivid recollection of the sight of my own bare
    arse as I open the gate of my Father's new house —
and step out into the road.

— ? —

A NAKED MAN IN A COUNTRY ROAD —
and heading towards Croyde Village —
but so Awake! —
so Aware! —
the slightest sound that might have been the footfall of a
    distantly oncoming pedestrian:
first glint over the brow of headlights:
I dive through the hedge into the field behind —
I flatten myself in the ditch —
uncaring of the scratches, the stings, the cuts —
the muck —
in fact delighting in it! —
and now I'm coming into the village itself —
and it's somewhat lamplit —
(there's a mist, but not a helpful mist,
it's a theatrical mist, a Macbeth mist —
creates mood but only comes up to your knees —
no Samurai could crouch that low —
a limbo dancer, maybe, but a skill that, not mine) —
and houses now and folk who live atop the shops.

— ? —

Best thing to do (it occurs to me) is to make myself
    IMPOSSIBLE OF ASPECT —

My Dad used to take me to the Crazy Gang Shows —
(Flannagan and Allen, Naughton and Gold, etc) —
and there was a bit of visual grammar peculiar to their shows:
if a Gang member's arsehole was touched up by a ladder, a
    rake, whatever, if he backed into the banisters —
this would trigger him into his own personal goosed-spesh
    eccentric walk —
and it was in a manner inspired by those memories, the Ministry
    of Funny Walks, Professor Walloffski, the Royal Ballet —
and my own nightmares —
that I progressed myself through Croyde Village.

My reasoning was this:
If someone came to their window, *Aghah!* yawned, saw me —
! —
They'd assume they were still asleep.

And now I'm outside the last shop in Croyde —
and it's the only interesting shop in Croyde —
it's the Shell Shop which sells the local and foreign shells —
and I have the courage (a light drizzle now) to linger at the Shell
    Shop window and pick my favourite exhibit:
the shell frog.

And then on and a left turn and down past the caravans and
    onto the beach —
and on the beach I hear voices —

and I fancy these are of the bodied variety and so I give them a
    wide berth, and then I'm at the sea, and I have a sensible
    swim in the sea —
(bracing how the salt bites into the wounds I'd received in the
    hedgerows) —
and out of the sea and across the wide beach and up the cliff
    walk this time and over the road —
and hop back in through the window —
and the Voice says: 'OK now?'

And the only answer I could give was:
'I've never in my life felt better.'

And I told no-one of these things for many years —
But then I was in Frankfurt, in the Café Fundus, and I'm
    drinking Himbiergeist in iced glasses with an artist called
    Hans —
and I tell him —
and then Hans tells me his story:
Three years previously (Hans telling me his story) he'd been
    living in the South of Germany in the small town of Pee —
'Of PEE!?' —
and then I realized what he was doing —
in the manner of Thomas Hardy and Edgar Allan Poe he was
    giving me the initial letter of the place (not 'Pee' but
    'P___') —
but I'd never heard anyone TALK like that —
'So you're living in P___, Hans?' —
(What secrets now?)

Hans had a studio in P____ —
and he'd set himself a courageous artistic challenge —
he'd stitched canvas together to the exact dimensions of the
    Bayeux Tapestry —
but not to knit and sew us something, no —
he was an oil painter, surreal, science-fictional —
and here's how he was going about it:
every night at midnight he'd step out from his studio and he'd
    walk the streets of P____, he'd walk 'em and walk 'em, for
    hours, till it comes to him which part of the mighty canvas he
    is to attack that night, and then he returns to the studio and
    paints through the night until his vision is completed or he
    falls apart exhausted —
and then the next night's prowl round P____.

— ? —

And it's early morning hours and Hans is out round P____ and
    he hears from the Voice and the Voice says to Hans:
'Move the stones' —
and Hans doesn't understand the instruction and it comes again:
    'Move the stones' —
and this time Hans is outside someone's front garden and there
    is a large and curious rock in there and perhaps it wants
    moving —
and he scrabbles it up and once he's got it in his arms IT'S
    TELLING HIM WHERE IT WANTS TO GO —
and it's round the corner and in someone else's garden —
and he's about to go and then he hears from another stone —
and that's what he's doing now, every night round P____ —
HE'S MOVING THE STONES.

— ? —

Sometimes he's merely twisting them —
turning them, re-pointing them in situ —
other times he's devoting a whole night to one stone's
　　considerable journey —
(For particularly large rocks which required a distant relocating
　　he would use his niece's pram.)

— ? —

And it's all having magic effect on the mighty opus —
things are moving apace on the great canvas —
and then he's picked up for it by the Polizei of P____.

— ? —

Ach so and *und so weiter* and it turns out that stone moving
　　isn't much of a crime —
but for Hans's own protection it's felt that he should now turn
　　his talents toward jig-saws and basket-weaving in a supervised
　　environment —
and he's in this place four weeks and then he's called up to see
　　the 'Fat Important Man' —
And the Fat Important Man takes a deal of interest in Hans and
　　his art and his ideas and his life and then there's a long pause
　　and the Fat Important Man goes out comes back in with a big
　　cigar and fools around cutting it and lighting it and then he
　　asks Hans this:
'Have you a commission?'

— ? —

The question asked in conspiratorial tones —
What is he really asking? —

The Fat Important Man? —
('Have you a commission?')
Hans didn't know —
but he answered: 'Yes'.

— ☉ —

And the Fat Important Man bows slightly and he apologizes to
    Hans that he's been kept in there so needlessly and so long —
and he helps Hans pack —
and he waves Hans onward with his 'commission' and wishes
    him all the best —
But when Hans gets back to his studio, he decides to remove
    himself forever from the small town of P____ —
and go live in the large city of F____.

— ☉ —

TWO

Have you a commission? —
HAVE YOU A COMMISSION? —
The way Hans reported it I'd found it stirring —
Have you a commission? —
in any event it's a good tip —
If you're ever in that circumstance and the guy asks you if
    you've got a commission say YES! —
But handy if you actually had one —
If I were ever to have one it would surely have something to do
    with the Dream:
'ENORMOUS SWIMMING BATH
VEGETATION AND FOLIAGE IN IT' —
(Imagine this: one night, in a dream, the Bard of Avon hits on
    his finest so far and wakes himself up and supposes himself to
    be quilling down the necessary notes of the vision —
Next morning he reads what he's written:
'CASTLE
SCANDINAVIA
BLOKE IN TIGHTS'.)

— ? —

And page 98 —
(*The Dawn of Magic*) —
just above where I wrote 'Enormous swimming bath etc.' —
this (a quotation):

'I have spent much time thinking about the alleged pseudo-
relations that are called coincidences. What if some of them
should not be coincidences?' —
turning back a few pages to find who said that —
Charles Fort —
an American author of the twenties and thirties —
who'd written 'The crack-pot's *Golden Bough*' —
he was:
'One of the monstrosities of literature' —
'To read Charles Fort is like taking a ride on a comet' —
'Sends you reeling against the doors which open onto something
other' —
but Pauwels and Bergier had only read one book by Charles
Fort, *The Book of the Damned* —
in a footnote on page 95 they tell us another they've heard of —
LO! —
they'd heard that really was fantastic —
so this was the tip then —
towards my commission —
Get *LO!*

— ❓ —

I went to Foyle's and they were abusive —
Second-hand bookshops now —
Specialists in the Arcane —
London and environs —
and it's not till I get to Birmingham that I meet a man who's
heard of it —
and it's not till I get to Newcastle-upon-Tyne that I meet a man
who reckons he once had one —
and years are passing —
and I've given up the hunt —
and then I'm asked to direct a Canadian Comedy show —
and I'm in Toronto.

— ❓ —

And I'm trying to cast the thing —
and I'm not finding it easy —
I'm beginning to think that 'Canadian Comedy Show' might be a
   contradiction in terms —
(like 'Military Intelligence') —
and then one morning comes in this young tubby
   Newfoundlander, Andy Jones, and he had thick glasses that
   made his eyes look bulgy like a frog's, and he was funny, and
   I thought: 'We're OK now; just build the show round Andy
   Jones' and that afternoon I'm in the W. H. Smith's of
   Toronto —
and this is how it happened:
I was attracted by a large format book of old sepia photographs
   of Red Indians, taken in the 1880s, but it was up high, too
   high for me, and so I moved a cardboard box over to stand
   on, and my foot slipped and ripped open the box —
and inside were *Complete Works*es of Charles Fort.

— ❓ —

I am holding the treasure —
I allow it to open where IT will —
I read —
how —
Ladies! —
If you kiss a frog —
and make a regular practice of this —
(morning and evening I think was the recommended regimen
   here) —
and if the frog starts to look a bit dicky you must choose the
   most robust of his tadpoles and get kissing that —
And if you feel that soon you may be departing this vale of
   tears —

you must pass the practice on to your daughter —
and so it must go —
on through the generations —
the centuries —
but in the end —
says Fort —
YOU WILL COME UP WITH A PRINCE.

— ❼ —

And Fort's pseudo proof of this is a cup of tea:
Is not the tea at the very edge of the cup slightly more cuppish
    than the stuff in the middle? —
And is not the interior of the cup not a load more teaish than
    the outer part and the handle? —
Well, damn right, and I bought the book —
but, something about it, that book, and I didn't open it again
    while I was in Canada —
put it safely in my case —
and eventually back to London with it —
and still unopened further I put it pride of place on the
    bookshelf.

— ❼ —

And I also brought back with me Andy Jones because I thought
    people might like to laugh at him over here.

— ❼ —

My feelings about thinking at this time (1972) —
I held there to be a difference between 'I think' and 'it occurs to
    me that . . .' —

Thinking is a step by step affair —
Whereas —
'It occurs to me that . . .' —
Well sometimes the most extraordinary things may, unbidden,
   occur.

— ❓ —

And it was late one night and something was unbidden
   occurring —
and it was coming in in the form of an epic dramatic poem —
and I was writing it down as it came in and it was looking really
   good and I knew all I had to do was KEEP OUT OF THE
   WAY! —
and it had a curious set-up to it:
it was set in 1948/49 in the Dagenham/Chadwell Heath area —
and the heroes were these two guys and I think one of them was
   an ex-prisoner of war who'd not returned at the time of
   repatriation, and his younger mate, a young Dagenham lad,
   and these two were so into Red Indian culture that —
well they were unemployable —
but they'd developed interesting abilities —
they could decide their next action by reading cigarette
   smoke —
sometimes they'd go to the station in order to listen to the
   babblings of the winos and the shopping-bag ladies in the
   belief that one time in the jabber they'd pick out a spirit
   message from Mighty Manitou —
and they were into litter-divination —
they would, as it were, I Ching litter bins —
'Close cover before striking' is an answer if you've asked the
   question —
'Keep Dry and Away From Children' —
sometimes a motto for the day like:
'Courage's bitter' —

(I recently saw a hoarding, I think it was advertising a new-style
  thinking men's magazine: 'Measure your Manhood Without a
  Ruler' —
I think they'd have liked that.)

— ❷ —

I'm going to bother you with the last short section of the epic
  dramatic poem as it was coming in —
This bit is called: 'THE COMING OF NSCHO-TCHI':

> 'In the Tavern by the Tram-Stop
> Heroes on the dark fire-water'

(which is Guinness) —

> 'One pint, two, then three and four
> "See the moon!" cries Appanatshka
> "Moon is twice as big as usual
> Sign that something big will happen
> Night of nights that moon portends!"
> In that instant comes a Lady
> Lady with the Long Black Hair
> "May I sit here" says the Lady
> Sits down on adjoining chair —
> Heroes speechless, stare in wonder
> Stare at Lady's long black hair —
> *"Das ist Nscho-Tchi, Appanatshka!*
> *Das ist Nscho-Tchi ist ganz klar!"*
> (*and as they stare at her three ectoplasmic*
> *feathers rise up behind her head*)
> Full of panic hunt the heroes
> Hunt for clues for what to do —
> Beer-mats, bottles, peanut packets —
> Nothing written what to do!
> Lady gripped by fit of shudders
> "Ooo" she cries, then "Agh" and "O" —

"My brothers brave I bring you blessings
But I feel funny; I must go!" —
Up she goes and out the door (*slam*)
Falls under a passing Tram—'

And sod it! – I wrote that last line! —
'Falls under a passing Tram' —
No she didn't do that —
I'd got in the way! —
and I'd shut off the transmission.

I tried to put my mind back into the receptive state it had
   presumably been in when the stuff was coming through —
but all I got was one sentence —
'HE WENT FOR AN ICE-CREAM IN THE INTERVAL' —
(He went for an ice-cream in the interval?) —
Suddenly I understood the meaning of that sentence:
It was the last time we saw Father! —
(I'm a seven-year-old little girl and my name is Maisie) —
We'd gone for a family outing to the Cinema —
we'd seen the first feature and then we wanted ice-creams and
   Dad had gone off to get the ice-cream —
THE END —
We know no more! —
We never saw him again —
Often we think of Father —
o yes often! —
we're haunted by the fucker! —
Better if he'd died of a stroke —
than that —
HE WENT FOR AN ICE-CREAM IN THE INTERVAL.

And so what does this mean apropos the Epic Poem? —
She doesn't fall under a tram she —
DISAPPEARS —
SHE VANISHES —
and the *Complete Works* of Charles Fort fell off the book shelf.

— ❓ —

And once I had it in my hand I knew what it was doing there! —
You know that bit about kissing frogs? —
I thought: 'I'll nick that!' —
I'll ring it a bit and use it as an invocation to Nscho-Tchi —
And then I thought this book has only ever been opened at that
    particular page and there must be predilection in the volume
    to open there again if only I can feel where it most wants to
    open.

— ❓ —

But it didn't open at the Frog-Kissing page —
in fact I'll tell you something weird:
I've now combed through the *Complete Works* of Charles Fort
    many times and —
THAT BIT ABOUT KISSING FROGS ISN'T IN IT —
This is what I found myself reading:
(Chapter 16 of *LO!*) —

> 'He walked around the horses.
> Upon Nov. 25 1809, Benjamin Bathurst, returning from
> Vienna, where, at the Court of the Emperor Francis, he
> had been representing the British Government, was in
> the small town of Perleberg, Germany. In the presence
> of his valet and his secretary, he was examining horses,
> which were to carry his coach over more of his journey

back to England. Under observation, he walked around
to the other side of the horses. He vanished.
For details see the *Cornhill Magazine*, pages 55–279.'

— ❷ —

And it's all coming in again —
and a fine invocation to Nscho-Tchi is dictated:

' "Long time we no see Nscho-Tchi
Nscho-Tchi where are you today?
We see you by the shining waters
See you in your plumes and braid
You who spoke the speech of chipmunks
(As do all daughters of the Moon)
You who bathed in laughing waters —
Nscho-Tchi come and see us soon!
You will know us tho' our feathers
Lie in drawers most of the day —
Now we only don the raiment
Very hidden, private times —
But, Nscho-Tchi you will know us —
Enter soon our love-sent rhymes . . ." '

And then as before:

'In the Tavern by the Tram-Stop
Heroes on the dark fire-water
"See the moon' Etc
. . . "Night of nights that moon portends!"
. . . comes a Lady
Lady with the Long Black Hair . . .
"May I sit here?" . . .
(*three ectoplasmic feathers* . . .)
. . . Nothing written what to do!
Lady gripped by fit of shudders

"Ooo" she cries, then "Agh" and "O" —
"My brothers brave I bring you blessings
But I feel funny; I must go!"
Schwupps!
'*Mein Gott, sie ist verschwunden!*' —
She who was there now has gone —
Into thin air she has vanished
Teleported miles away . . .
She now appears in North Alaska
On the White Man's "Dawson Trail" . . .
Meanwhile in Tavern wail the heroes
Rend the room with shrieks of loss —
Worried waiter brings fire-water
Brings them crisps and rolls and nuts —
In snow-white froth of dark fire-water
Read they the sign of where she's gone . . .
In the night she freezes solid
Statue Queen in Land of Gold —
But colder still than lonely Ice-Queen
Are the hearts of our two heroes:
They were young men,
                              now they're old.'

— ❓ —

And then with the satisfaction that I'd helped something
    remarkable into the world, I retired to bed —
and there was a silence —
more than mere quiet —
a devouring silence —
the silence was devouring the creaks and bumps and ticks which
    are proper to the night —
it had eaten away, even, the sound of my own ears —
and in that silence my mind kept playing over and re-playing
    what seemed a somewhat singular event of the evening:

What was that bit? —
He went for an ice-cream in the interval —
and I'd deduced he'd disappeared and then so she doesn't fall
    under a tram, she vanishes, and then Fort falling off the book
    shelf (but Man! it hadn't 'fallen' off at all it had sailed off the
    book shelf as if KICKED BY A TINY FOOT!) —
so there must be – it's obvious – there must be – a —
non-physical entity —
a 'fairy' if you will —
whose special subject is 'Enchanted Vanishment' —
and she was so tickled that I was going to be writing on her
    subject that she'd given this helpful kick to things.

— ? —

And I asked myself this: 'Well then, Kenneth, do you think
    people ever do just . . . vanish?' —
And my answer was 'YES! I do' —
and then I thought: 'Yeah, and I bet it's when you're as clear as
    this about it YOU GO!' —
and then a worse thought: 'Yeah, and I bet it's when you think
    you're as clear as this about it that you THINK YOU'VE
    GONE.'

— ? —

Try to shake the idea out of my head —
think about where I might go on holiday —
but I can't fool it —
(what?) —
there's a demand —
(inside me? outside me? I don't know) —
that I devote full mind to Vanishment —
Try to fight it! —

Fill the mind with Abstract Blackness —
not easy —
(possibly not possible) —
Maybe if I can recall specific black items —
black shoes —
black stockings —
black bin bags —
black toy train —
AND I'M WINNING —
but then I'm aware that every orifice of my body —
(and I refer here too to secondary orifices —
the nipples, the button thing in the middle of the tum) —
all my orifices have become worms —
ALIEN WORMS WITH TEETH —
and bent on vigorous self-ingurgitation.

— ? —

With will —
I attempt to draw all this orificular aggravation away —
and into the centre of the MIND —
and then I knew —
why cultures world-wide —
and going back centuries —
have always held that with certain mental states —
the only answer is to —
BORE A HOLE IN THE HEAD.

— ? —

The following morning I rose late —
I could find no clothes that suited my mood so I put none on —
I devoted some hours to bizarre experimentation like finding out
   actually how long you could take to make a cup of coffee —

whether I could read the mail without opening the envelopes —
But later, sometime after three in the afternoon, I was at work.

— ❓ —

I'd taken the *Complete Works* of Charles Fort into the toilet —
Chapter 16 of *LO!*, I read on —
HE RAN INTO THE MILL —
'Chicago Tribune, Jan. 5, 1900 – "Sherman Church, a young
   man employed in the Augusta Mills (Battle Creek, Mich.) has
   disappeared. He was seated in the Company's office, when he
   arose and ran into the mill. He has not been seen since. The
   mill has been almost taken to pieces by the searchers, and the
   river, woods, and country have been scoured, but to no avail.
   Nobody saw Church leave town, nor is there any known
   reason for his doing so." '
Ambrose Bierce, author of the *Devil's Dictionary*
   disappeared —
Fort writes:
'I wonder whether Ambrose Bierce ever experimented with
   self-teleportation. Three of his short stories are of
   "mysterious disappearances". He must have been
   uncommonly interested to repeat so.' —
And on into Chapter 17:
'One is snoring along, amidst the ordinary marvels of dream-
   land – and there one is, naked, in a public place, with no
   impression of how one got there. I'd like to know what
   underlies the prevalence of this dream, and its
   disagreeableness, which varies, I suppose, according to one's
   opinion of oneself. I think that it is sub-conscious awareness
   of something that has often befallen human beings, and that
   in former times was commoner. It may be that occult
   transportations of human beings do occur, and that, because
   of their selectiveness, clothes are sometimes not included.' —
'Naked in the street – strange conduct by a strange man.' . . .

Early in the evening of January 6th (1914) – 'weather
bitterly cold – a naked man appeared, from nowhere that
could be found out, in High Street, Chatham.' And 'I have
records of six persons, who, between Jan. 14, 1920, and Dec.
9, 1923, were found wandering in or near the small town of
Romford, Essex, England, unable to tell how they got there,
or anything about themselves.'

— ❷ —

And 'bizarre arrival of things' —
Apport of objects —
and then it came to me —
(why had my mind blanked it out) —
it had only been less than three weeks before —
THE SAGA OF THE KEYS! —
About seven in the evening —
decide I'll got to the pub —
feel for keys —
can't find keys —
there's been trouble with keys before —
if I put my keys anywhere I put them in the kitchen drawer —
if they're not in my pants pocket they're in the kitchen
    drawer —
but they're not in the kitchen drawer —
not in my pants pocket and not in the kitchen drawer —
and not on the hook —
I'm hunting through the pockets of pants I haven't worn for a
    year —
two pairs of pants I don't even recognize —
and they're not in the kitchen drawer and they're not on the
    hook and not in the pants and they're not by the bed —
looking in jackets now —
perhaps I've become the sort of person who puts his keys in
    jackets —
Kitchen Drawer: No —
Hook: No —
By the Bed: No —

Mac—Overcoat —
No—No! —
and I'm back in front of the kitchen drawer again —
And I shriek at it:
FUCKING KEYS BE IN THERE —
!!! —
Thank you —
off to the pub.

— ? —

This is how *LO!* begins:
'A naked man in a city street – the track of a horse in volcanic
  mud – the mystery of reindeer's ears – a huge black form like
  a whale, in the sky, and it drips red drops as if attacked by
  celestial swordfishes – an appalling cherub appears in the
  sea —
Confusions.
Showers of frogs and blizzards of snails – gushes of periwinkles
  down from the sky —
The preposterous, the grotesque, the incredible – and why, if I
  am going to tell of hundreds of these, is the quite ordinary so
  regarded?'
Note Fort's use of the hyphen —
LO! has more hyphens than any book I know —
(although I may just top it in this one) —
and somewhere he tells us why:
It's Fort's opinion that everything in the Universe is linked with
  everything else —
so a Full Stop is a Lie —
Or a Hyphen coming straight at you.

— ? —

'An unclothed man shocks a crowd – a moment later, if nobody
  is generous with an overcoat, somebody is collecting

handkerchiefs to knot around him. A naked fact startles a
meeting of a scientific society – and whatever it has for loins is
soon diapered with conventional explanations . . . The
Princess Caraboo tells of herself, a story, in an unknown
language, and persons who were themselves liars have said
that she lied, though nobody has ever known what she told
. . . – and where Cagliostro came from, and where he went,
are so mysterious that only historians say they know – . . . An
onion and a lump of ice – and what have they in common?'
Is this any regular way to write a book? —
Not essay style is it —
not poem —
my feeling —
growing —
was —
INVOCATION.

— ❓ —

And at that moment there's a knock at the door and I decide to
 answer it —
(drape myself in the dog's blanket) —
Two actors at the door, Mark Weill and David Stockton, and
 their first words are:
'Andy Jones has disappeared.'

— ❓ —

I say, 'Come in' —
I say, 'I think something's trying to teach me something' —
and I don't let them speak —
and I give them each a piece of paper and a pen and I say to
 write down, independently, no conferring, exactly what they
 mean by —
ANDY JONES HAS DISAPPEARED.

— ❓ —

And they'd been rehearsing Andy's show pub hours in the
  Falcon in the King's Cross area —
and they'd been turfed out at 3:20 and Andy had said that he
  had to go to the toilet —
and so he'd gone down into the public convenience —
Mark and David waiting for him at the top —
and quite a long time had gone by —
and so they'd gone down to hurry him up —
and when they'd got down there —
THERE WAS NO-ONE THERE.

I say, 'Listen it's like I've been signed up for a course at the
  Invisible College,' and I tell them about falling under the
  tram, and going for an ice-cream at the interval, and Bathurst
  teleporting off from behind his horses, and the fairy kicking
  Fort off the book shelf, and Mark says:
'I think we should go to the Police.'

And Ah! and that's a dilemma and Yes! I can see that the Police
  might help us find Andy but really, I'm sure of this:
if we go rushing off to the cops at this point I'm going to be
  crossed off the register of the Phantom Academy —
so I say, 'Let's just call the Prophet in first' —
And this was agreed to.

The Prophet was an extraordinary guy who'd moved in up the
  road —

He styled himself 'Protean Synthesist' —
and if you asked him a question —
you know those Hindu Gods and Goddesses that have the extra
    arms coming out of their elbows, shoulders, wherever? —
well, if you asked the Prophet a question it was as if with his
    many arms he was reaching into remote and remarkable
    libraries of world culture —
(he'd be speed-reading locked grimoires on your behalf) —
and he'd always give you an answer that no-one else could —
and, Yes, he'd come right over.

— ❓ —

When I heard his knock I'm straight to the door —
I want to test him —
Will he be up to THIS occasion? —
I say: 'Prophet! Andy Jones has disappeared and we think it's a
    "round the horses" job' —
PROPHET: (MANY ARMS REACHING INTO REMOTE
    LIBRARIES) . . . Benjamin Bathurst? —
YES!—Prophet, you passed! and now unloading all on the
    Prophet:
Thinking, occurring, ice-cream, fairy;
LO!, keys, Invocation, Andy Jones; —
and Mark (freaking) says: 'What's going on!?' —
And the Prophet says: 'Boys, do you listen to nothing that I tell
    you? The real nature of the Universe is unknown and
    unknowable! – Your problem is that your World-Reality
    Picture is based on half-ingested Science! – These so-called
    Scientific Laws aren't laws at all! – They weren't given to
    some bearded Gent on a Mountain Top! – They're mere
    observations on how it usually goes! – There is only one word
    in the English language which approximates the true nature of

the Universe and that word is "OTHER"! – and every little once in a while THE OTHER WILL MANIFEST and it's good to be around at those times, because, if ye've the courage – THERE MAY BE SOMETHING UP FOR GRABS!' —
and Mark says: 'I think we should go to the Police.'

— ② —

'For sure,' (Prophet taking the case) 'we could go to the Police – and what are we going to tell them? – What've we got for them? – there's Kenneth's visit from the "Library Angel" and it'll be our duty, will it not, to draw attention to the bizarre synchronicity that Kenneth is reading what he holds to be incantatory literature in his lav and teleports Andy Jones out of his toilet – what else have we got to give them on which to base their enquiries? —
and if we go in telling them these things —
I think we'll be all right —
I don't think we'll be arrested —
But I'm fucking sure we'll be put on a list.'

— ② —

And Mark says: 'Well let's go and look for him' —
'For sure, we can go and look for him,' says the Prophet,
'. . . but statistically, in cases of bizarre removal, one is quicker to be united with the victim if one just goes severely about one's business; and then, if what we all hope happens, happens, that Andy Jones is returned to flesh-form in the Camden Town area, he'll have something to return to – you two,' (Mark and David) 'if you weren't here what would you be doing?' —

Mark said: 'Well we might be doing anything now, but in half an
   hour we'd be rehearsing again' —
The Prophet said: 'So go rehearse.'

— ☉ —

And Mark and David went and I asked the Prophet this:
'Do you think what we have here with Andy Jones is an actual
   case of "round the horses" teleportation?' —
And the Prophet said: '. . . No.'

— ☉ —

'No,' he said, 'what you've got here, I compute, is a case of
   Invisibility!' —
'Invisibility?!' —
Apparently Invisibility is merely a matter of being able to hide
   in front of things —
'How does that work?'
'I've told you, haven't I,' said the Prophet, 'about the
   fourteenth-century Japanese Spy-Courier Monks?' —
'I dunno . . . you may have . . .' —
Evidently, an article in a recent *Lancet* had vindicated the early
   work in this field by the fourteenth-century Japanese Spy-
   Courier Monks – Experiments had been done on the eye-balls
   of newly-hatched ducklings – and the muscles of their tiny
   eye-balls had responded to the shape of PREDATORY birds
   flying overhead, but had in no way responded to the shapes of
   starlings, pigeons or Concorde —
'And as it was with the ducklings, so it is with us,' said the
   Prophet —
'From the moment we are hatched from our mother's womb the
   muscles of our eye-balls are ready, from that first moment, to
   RESPOND TO THE SHAPE WHICH THREATENS –

thus – if you can train yourself to progress yourself in a
series of BIZARRELY UN-ALARMING POSTURES, you
can by-pass the muscles of the human eye . . .' —
And the Prophet waved me Goodbye —
With his many arms.

— ❓ —

And yet —
Isn't the Prophet there, (great man), explaining one miracle
    with two? —
Go back to Andy Jones in the public convenience —
in his cubicle —
finishing off —
now coming up the metal stairs —
Let's say he's 'adjusting his dress' and in so doing he happens to
    hit one of those bizarrely un-alarming postures thus
    by-passing the muscles of Mark and David's eye-balls! —
BUT THEN THEY TOO MUST HAVE BEEN LOLLING
    ABOUT IN BIZARRELY UN-ALARMING POSTURES
    WHICH BY-PASSED THE MUSCLES OF THE
    EYE-BALLS OF ANDY JONES! —
(I give you the Prophet's explanation —
it may give comfort to some —
I tell you this:
if you feel you may have been responsible for the teleportation
    of a treasured chum it gives you pause.)

— ❓ —

I wasn't to hear from the Voice for sixteen years —
(dating from the teleportation of Andy Jones) —
I'd found a lost bit of London —
(actually my dog found it) —

Only those who know it know it —
The Valley beneath Stamford Hill —
and the Abbey National and I bought a modest house there —
Step round the corner and onto the tow-path —
(Tow-path of the Navigation Cut of the River Lea) —
and do you believe you're in London, friend; look on the back
    of that old man's bike —
that wooden box on the back with a cabbage and some onions in
    it —
he's just picked them from his allotment! —
that's a heron! —
You just missed them but they were cormorants! —
(Tottenham's up to the left, we're walking to the right) —
passed my neighbours who live on the narrow boats —
the rowing club —
The Rowing Club Café —
also known as George's Café and it's been a caff for ninety
    years, and the first time I went inside I thought I was *déjà
    vu*ing:
it was a little like the club-house pavilion of the Valentine's
    Tennis and Social Club at Gants Hill —
and my Father had been secretary of that club when I was seven
    or so —
and George was selling those post-war cakes I hadn't seen for
    thirty or more years:
puff pastry jobs, with icing sugar on the top and noodles of
    coconut embedded in the icing-sugar, and something a wee bit
    sinister in the middle.

— ❓ —

And then I'd gone way back:
I was about seven, and I'm playing on the floor of the
    Valentine's Tennis Club Pavilion, and my Father's sitting at a
    table writing whatever it is he has to write in his enormous

ledger and there are only two other people in there, a male
member, beginning to bald, and he's teaching a new young
lady member how to play darts and he's exciting her with this
piece of information: 'You don't hold your dart like this as
you'd think', he's saying, showing his dart pointing towards
the board, 'but like this', point downwards, and he throws off
his three demonstration darts and goes to the board to
retrieve them, and the girl says, 'What like this?', and the guy
turns round – like a Red Indian – with this dart sticking in the
top of his head – and the girl is shrieking – but he doesn't
know what she's shrieking at – he can't feel anything! – and
my Dad looks up, and he takes in the scene in one, and he
shoos the hysterical female into the Ladies Changing Room
and then he says to the bloke: 'You just sit down there.
You've had a bit of an accident. Don't touch your head!' And
the ambulance came and under medical supervision the dart
was removed and the bloke was fine —
Well, actually he was subject to occasional winking fits.

— ? —

And in George's caff you'll be likely to encounter Ken Kelly —
a gravel-voiced old-timer of the River —
Kelly is the only person who has an actual permit to LIVE on
  his boat —
and that's because his time on the Lea goes way back —
way back before the Marina and all that nonsense —
Ken Kelly can recall the BROTHEL BOATS OF THE LEA! —
and he'll recall them for you most mornings over breakfast.

— ? —

There's a footbridge by George's which goes over to the Marina —
but we'll stay on the tow-path till we get to the quaint old white
  metal footbridge —

and we go over that and we're on Walthamstow Marsh —
to a pond —
and I'm having to cross this bridge and go to this pond every
    day —
because my little old mongrel dog has a commission.

— ? —

This is her commission:
she has to get all the over-night crap out of this particular
    pond —
(this pond was formed overnight by a doodle-bug, just like me,
    and maybe the same doodle-bug, date and geography offer it
    as a possibility) —
I don't throw sticks in for her —
she just plunges straight in and gets out any cans and crap —
(After that hurricane, wow, she was magnificent, she's only a
    slight little mongrel, but she found, in the water, she could
    move trees.)

— ? —

One morning, about thirty yards from the pond —
I could just see it through the grasses and coppice —
a picnic table of heavy wood, with heavy wood benches —
investigation —
the legs and supports are sunk deep into the ground —
definitely wasn't there yesterday —
and I don't like it —
it spoils the illusion I am 'Stalker' —
in the Zone.

— ? —

And days go by —
and every day I'm passing it —
and I never see anyone sitting at it —
and then one morning I sit at it —
and I think:
I know why it's been put here:
It's to be my Office.

— ❓ —

It was the first of that freak terrific weather —
(We've allowed all this pollution to invade the skies and the
    result is terrific weather —
a shame to waste it) —
and with the invention of the Cellnet telephone, do we need the
    walls and ceilings? —
? —
My Marsh Office —
this maybe qualifies as a Social Invention —
and I want to be interviewing people here —
I must get back into big cast theatre productions again —
I want all those actresses and people writing in with their c.v.s
    and photos —
and I'll send them the relevant pages of the London *A-Z*,
    marking George's caff as the place to report in —
and no-one to meet them —
they can have a cup of tea —
chance one of the cakes —
then in comes Ken Kelly —
Corncrake voice: 'Any thespians 'ere?' —
Kelly ushers you out and onto his old boat —
ships you off down river —
moors up under the Marsh bridge —
Captain Kelly looks about —
sniffs the air —

'Don't seem to want yer yet' —
Kelly scarpering the nine cats off the teapot —
some danger he's going to make you a cup of tea —
but from the office I let off a 506 Naval Distress Flare —
'Oo 'e's callin' for yer nah!' —
Ken Kelly pulls out a machete —
hacks a new path for you through the marsh grass —
then you get your first sight of me —
in my Marsh Office —
swinging deals on my Cellnet —
'Just sit down there—I'll be with you in a minute.'

I'd get all this together and then it'd piss down —
but the answer is all along the banks of the Lea —
what I need is one of those enormous fisherman's umbrellas —
George says to go to Don's Fishing Tackle Emporium in
    Edmonton off the North Circular.

Don's —
(Fishing tackle is mysterious and daunting) —
'Yes, sir?' —
Don presumably —
'I'm looking for one of those large fisherman's umbrellas
    please' —
'A 48 or a 51?' —
? —
'Erm – I'm not sure – you see I'm not a – it won't be for fishing –
    I've got an office on the Marsh – and I don't want my typing
    getting wet if it, er . . .' —

'Very healthy, the outdoors' says Don —
'Well is there a difference in price between the 48s and the
    51s?' —
'Yes sir – the 48s are cheaper because the 51s are bigger' —
I see a rack of them —
taking one out —
'What's this? Is this a 48?' —
'Yes, sir' —
'Can I see it up?' —
Enormous – it'd take up the whole width of the pavement —
48's ok for me —
then I find the extending prong attachment in the stem —
'the prong arrangement – is that any longer on the 51s?' —
'No, sir, the prong arrangement is uniform on all models' —
It's £28 —
I see an umbrella in the rack marked '£10' —
'Is this a 48?' —
'Yes, sir, but that's nylon' —
'Ah, nylon not as good as – this?' —
'Well, no, sir, in a mighty deluge you'll get a light mist under
    there' —
'O, well, no, that's no good for me, I'll have the first one' —
And then I find these marvellous fishing waistcoats —
WITH POCKETS ON THE POCKETS —
I'll have to have one of these —
just the job for a man with an office on the marsh —
(you can fit into the main pocket the *Complete Works* of Charles
    Fort) —
and I'm suddenly aware Don has a pretty young lady assistant
    and she's standing right by me, and she says: 'Have you really
    got an office on the Marsh?' —
'Oh, yes – got me little portable typewriter, me Cellnet –' —
PRETTY ASSISTANT: (CALLING OVER TO DON) 'You
    know your stuff gets used for all sorts of things – you know
    the big fishing-tackle boxes?' —
'Yes, I know, the BBC use them for make-up' —

'Yes, I know that, but as well the Women's Institute use them
   for competitive cake-making' —
(I don't feel I've ushered in one of Don's favourite days) —
ME: 'Anyway, I'd like one of these waistcoats' —
Don pointing at waistcoat: 'and 's not fer . . .' —
?—
'It's not for what?'
Don is pointing at a small square of fur on the top right of the
   coat —
'Snot Fur,' says Don, and mimes how, with your hands full of
   nets and rods, and it's a cold day, you can whisk away a dew-
   drop with your square of snot-fur.

Next morning in the Office, getting the feel of the fisherman's
   waistcoat —
thrilling to the possibilities of the many pockets —
it would be possible, it seemed to me, to stiffen the pockets on
   the pockets with thin wood strips —
and make them into drawers —
A Chest of Drawers! —
Interviewing some actress, I'd pull out a drawer in the waistcoat,
   take out an index card, take down her particulars, pull out
   another drawer, and file her in an alphabetic system —
and a drawer for stamps and envelopes —
a built in calculator —
Pictures of Loved Ones —
But what on earth SHOW am I interviewing these folk for? —
I couldn't think of any show amazing enough to warrant these
   sensational interviewing techniques.

But, sod it, let's just get on with the interviews —
Usually when you interview people, there you are, the Bollix,
   the Man with the Concept, and they have to prove and plead
   how they'll fit in —
these would be a new Marsh style of non-Fascistic interviews —
These techniques (grumpy Captain Kelly and his boat, the
   machete, the 506 distress flare, the Cellnet ringing constantly –
   I'd get a mate to keep ringing every three minutes during
   the interview – 'Well just try and keep it quiet and restrained,
   Donald, but I'll have to call you back, I'm seeing someone'—
   and not forgetting that the whole thing's taking place in the
   middle of a forgotten inner-urban wilderness!) would be likely
   to jolt the interviewee into the fabled 'awakened state' and
   he/she loose upon ME the Concept, or some strand of same.

And as I came down from that moment of fine inspiration —
I felt I was not alone —
Prettyboy Tentringer is about to pronounce:
(It is my assumption that PBT and the Voice are one and the
   same) —
'Yes . . .' said Voice Prettyboy, and then 'Hmmm' —
'What?' I said —
Eventually I got it out of him —
That I shouldn't bring any of my old life and business to this
   Office —
'In this Office on the Marsh you should do MARSH
   BUSINESS' —
'What do you mean?'
But he was gone —
He left me with that.

In this Office on the Marsh you should do Marsh Business.

What is the Business of the Marsh?

Be a Nature Poet?

Keep a Marsh Diary?

I was confused —
In this Office on the Marsh you should do Marsh Business.

I doubt if I would have ever got anything together regarding
    'marsh business' if it hadn't happened to be peculiarly cold
    one morning —
I was setting off for the doodle-bug pond so the dog could
    perform her commission, but the cold was biting into the
    brain and I had to return for my hat —
but I couldn't find my hat —
but then I found A hat —
a dirty, knitted woolly hat, with a pom-pom on it —
(I couldn't recall ever having entertained the wearer of this hat) —

but I stuck it on and took the dog off to the pond —
When I got back, hat still on, I saw myself in the mirror —
'God', I thought, 'I can't go out like this —
I look like a Smurf!' —
but something kept me staring at this image of myself in the
    mirror —
the hat had a crudely knitted emblem on its front, which seemed
    to be a dolphin in a Christmas party hat behaving
    pornographically with a banana —
and the longer I looked at myself in this hat —
the more confirmed of opinion I became —
that the Man Who Does Marsh Business on the Marsh —
HE WEARS THIS HAT!

— ? —

You've heard of a 'thinking-cap'? —
I think there may be literal truth in it —
many, who habitually wear a hat, confirm this:
take your hat off for a few minutes in a pub or somewhere and
    somebody will be putting it on – Women do this! —
and when they do so, nine times out of ten —
THEIR BEHAVIOUR WILL BE MODIFIED FOR THE
    BETTER! —
As I understand it, when you think, a measurable amount of
    electrical energy is produced —
is it not likely that some would lodge in hat-grease?

— ? —

I kept the hat on —
I slept in it —
and it started taking me places —
it found for me a quaint, back-street shop which specialized in
    very old bicycles —

and it had me buy a very old lady's bike —

it took me to the Church Book Boutique, which only opens on
Wednesday afternoons if the vicar feels like it, and we bought
Sex Life of the Flowers and J. G. Ballard's *The Day of
Creation* —

but when it had me buy twelve Chinese black and red note-
books I got the picture —

I was to be the PASSIVE PROTAGONIST —

In my Marsh Office I would detail the days as they fell in my
Marsh Journal —

sometimes I would be entering people's lives —

but subtly, peripherally, not enough to change them —

just enough to write about them —

the Guy Who is Around —

The Passive Protagonist —

The Man Who Does Marsh Business on the Marsh.

And came the appointed morning and I rose early and Chinese
notebook (now *Marsh Journal*, Vol I), *Sex Life of Flowers*
and Ballard's *Day of Creation* all easily contained in
fisherman's waistcoat pockets —

and I decided to take the 48 (even though it looked not at all
like rain) and I fully extended the prong and set off on the old
bike —

feeling terrific, like a Knight of Olde —

(but I had to go the long way round as I could only steer to the
left) —

and I settled myself in at the Office —

Marsh Business —

The Passive Protagonist —

What was going to happen? —

Today and everyday? —

In my hat.

— ? —

And I began the *Marsh Journal* and I wrote:
'THE OFFICE. 7.23 a.m. – It may be the first day of Spring –
   Man with two dogs carrying stick goes by – Birds twittering –
   Pigeon fluttering and briefly soaring –' —
and it was a fine morning and the sun was streaming past my
   face and I was noticing that my eyebrows have now
   overgrown so unruly that it's like I'm looking through a hedge
   at everything —
and I try an experiment —
I take out a couple of clothes pegs —
(many years ago I discovered clothes pegs to be a superior paper
   clip) —
and I pegged up my brows —
terrific! —
I don't need glasses, just pegs! —
(It's commercially inadvisable for me to trim my eyebrows as I
   sometimes pick up these little parts on the telly playing
   somebody who's just invented something) —
'Dog asleep, or dozing rather, in the dewy grass clumps – Bike
   leant against table' —
And then I could write no more —
because out of the bushes behind the pond, had appeared a
   young man whose body language was so alarming it would not
   have by-passed the eye-muscles of an idiot.

— ❓ —

And he had with him a plastic bag —
with some weight of substance at the bottom of it —
and he plunged his head into the bag and took an obscenely
   deep breath from it —
and then commenced kicking shit out of invisible people —
'Fuck! and Fuck! and Fuck Off! and Fuck!' —

and then he saw me —
and he paused —
and then he roared: 'Clothes PEGS!!!' —
and he delivered the word 'pegs' in THE SHOUT:
THE LEGENDARY NOISE WHICH KILLS RATS AT A
    HUNDRED YARDS.

— ❓ —

And I had heard [and suffered from] that noise before —
1970 when I had my touring comedy troupe, 'Ken Campbell's
    Roadshow' —
and we were honoured —
I was asked to address the Symposium of World Theatre —
all the theatre-producing nations of the world had sent two
    delegates to London's Old Vic —
except for the Philippine Islands who'd sent thirty-seven —
and I was on a panel with Max Stafford-Clark, still the Artistic
    Director of the Royal Court Theatre, Sloane Square, but then
    heading the Traverse's touring wing, and the bloke from the
    Welfare State Troupe —
the young hopefuls of British Theatre —
and hungry for World Tours we told the world about
    ourselves —
I think I may have over-intellectualized what we were about but
    I sought to repair that in my concluding statement: '. . . but
    often we just race into the venues like lunatics and take it
    from there' —
and we'd all said our say, and the Chairman asked the World if
    it had any questions —
and from its ranks rose this maniac Brit —
'Yes,' he said, 'I've got a question for Mr Campbell —
you say you race into your venues like lunatics —
why don't you race in like DIABETICS —
and vomit over your audience?' —

and when he hit that syllable 'bet of 'diaBETics' —
that's when he hit the RAT-KILLING TIMBRE —
and he got me in the knee with it —
and I rose to reply but my knee had no 'spannung' to it and I fell
    under the table —
this excited the maniac to further excess —
some World Delegates, nervous of terrorism, now leaving —
Maniac now coming up to the platform —
desperately trying to hold my knee together in a half hobble,
    half hop —
I flee the stage —
followed by Welfare State chap, Chairman —
Max Stafford-Clark, bravely, I thought at that moment, the last
    to leave, even attempting dialogue with the Maniac —
but then giving it up, and now joining us, and Max kind enough
    to escort me to the bar and buy me a large Scotch —
and then Max says:
'I'm sorry about my Father' —
and my voice came out and it was like a little boy's voice and it
    said:
'Was that your Dad? —
I didn't bring my Dad.'

— ❷ —

And now, once more, on the Marsh, that mythic bellow, and it's
    got me in the knee again —
and I rise and fall —
and gathering the books together, and my 48 —
and lurker now coming towards me —
waving bag of substance —
gait of Ancient Messenger on last legs —
and me holding knee and hopping round to bike —
and 'I'm only BREATHING' he says —
'just TRAINING' and he slaps himself ludicrously hard on the

chest, and crouches briefly presumably to persuade me he's
into ski-jump practice on the Marsh —
and he's got two teeth missing at the front —
and there's slobber on his chin —
and a pus-encrusted wart on his nose —
and stuck in it what looked like a snapped off cocktail stick.

— ? —

And I'm on the bike, with all impedimenta, wobbling off toward
    the river, dog following —
I fall off —
'You all right?' he calls —
'Yes, fine' – I wave him away —
and wheel the bike and stuff far out of range.

— ? —

A little sit —
a little rest by the river —
and then I get up and I'm testing my joints and they're not too
    bad —
and I had my 48 on my back, and I catch sight of my shadow —
and something about it brings to mind the Seven Samurai —
and I hear the Samurai music —
and I resolve to return —
we shall return.

— ? —

Back at the Office —
I decide not to write any more —
the Breather is in the bushes bag in hand —

I pose as a bloke reading Ballard's *Day of Creation* —
I say 'pose', I was just taking the sort of time it would take to
   get to the end of a page and turn it, and I am aware that the
   Breather is now standing over me —
'Is that your book?' he says —
'Yes' I say —
'Would like to see where it writes about me?' he says —
he takes the book as one who knows it well —
(he has put his bag of strange substance on the Office table) —
he is dribbling —
he shows me a name in the book:
'Chad' —
'Is that your name – "Chad"?' —
'Yeah' —
This is the sentence:
'Why not go to the Sudan, or Chad?' —
Chad became my first regular client in the Office.

I have seen into Chad's bag —
fumey, green-tinged putty —
in coils like an old brain —
One morning he tells me of his ambition:
to be a pop star —
but he had a dis-quiet about following his dream —
'Why do all singers go gay?' —
'I don't know,' said the Passive Protagonist, 'it is odd now you
   mention it – why do all singers go gay?' —
Well, if he was going to be a singer HE WASN'T GOING TO
   GO GAY! —
This lemming instinct of all singers to plunge themselves into the
   abyss of gaydom, frankly sickened him —
The Passive Protagonist encouraged him to give it a shot, hoping
   that the world would be ready for such a revolutionary
   approach —

'I mean trees aren't gay,' he said, 'you don't get gay trees –' —
The Passive P was tested here; now well into *The Sex Life of
    Flowers* he could have argued the point, but 'No,' he said,
    'trees aren't gay –' —
'Or ants –' —
he was peering down at some ants —
he thought long and dribbled a bit, then he said: 'Actually
    there's no telling with ants –' —
and it was a fine morning and he took a huge belt from his
    bag —
and the sun was streaming through his hair —
(and his teeth) —
and I sensed he had a vision coming on —
I gave him space to have it —
It came: 'It's like this, isn't it,' he said, 'it goes in here' (pointing
    at the mouth) 'as food . . . and then . . .' (long pause) 'it
    turds out –' —
'Hmmm –' I said, then: 'Wow!' —
'But what does it get up to while it's in you? YOU DON'T
    KNOW – I don't know and you don't know —
food could act in gay ways in your body, it could be acting in a
    gay way NOW AND YOU WOULDN'T KNOW IT —
Christ!' he said —
(bleakly, he put his head in his bag, and then emerging:) —
'A thought like that could obsess you to study up and become
    the greatest surgeon the world has ever known – and you'd
    cut yourself open to catch your food acting in gay ways but as
    soon as it saw you were looking – IT'D STOP DOING IT
    AND YOU'D NEVER KNOW!

— ❓ —

In lighter vein: 'Can you tickle yourself?' asked Chad —
'I don't think it's possible,' I said —
'For a successful bout of tickling the "to be tickled person" (or

"prospective ticklee") must not be able to predict the
   precise spots which are to be tickled' —
'Yeah?' he said —
and he put his head in his bag, and the instant he emerged he
   commenced tickling himself and cackling hysterically —
I was impressed.

It occurred to me that a semi-feral chap like Chad might have
   bizarre powers —
'Can you do things, Chad?' I asked —
'Like what?' he said, dubiously —
'I don't know,' I said, 'like make yourself invisible, make things
   appear, that sort of thing. . . ?' —
He looked at me a long time —
he disappeared his whole head into the bag —
this time it seemed he was not merely indulging in the fumes —
but looking directly into the old green brain for an answer —
when he came out he seemed to be remembering . . . something
   . . . he scrabbled up a stone and he put it on the Office
   table —
'I can move things,' he said, 'I could move that stone from there
   to there –' (indicating a distance of approximately four
   inches) —
'What, with the power of your mind?' —
'Yeah,' he said —
'Could you do it now?' —
He sat down at the table —
he focussed his powers on the stone —
minutes —
he sought further inspiration from the bag —
and then he remembered something else —
'Yeah!' he said, 'yeah – I could move it – I COULD! – but if I
   did, the smell it would make would be APPALLING!'

In the Office, evening approaching —
and suddenly, Chad —
and he says: 'Have you ever been in a filter bed?' —
'No?' I said —
'Are you up to it?' he says —
'OK' – having no idea what this adventure might entail.

— ❓ —

And it's on, Chad leading, further south down the tow-path of
    the Lea —
under the railway viaduct, under the last two arches of which, in
    the early 1900s Alliott Verdon Roe (Avro) had his
    workshops, and but a few weeks after Kitty Hawk had his
    motorbike engined tri-plane rising nine foot off the ground,
    thus pioneering Britain's first powered manned flight over
    Walthamstow Marshes —
and then, Avro and butler-cum-mechanic into the riverside
    tavern, the Anchor and Hope, there to spend the night telling
    the tale —
The Anchor and Hope, where to this day, the stranger is
    greeted with bright eyes —
regulars vie to have you, and not to turn you over, not
    usually —
have no fear of those unshaven faces —
something there —
the slow flowing water of the Lea? —
contemplation of the Marshes across? —
local deity? —
is it built on a conjunction of ley-lines? —
or is it Avro's return which is subconsciously awaited? —
but something keeps always, whatever the weather, several
    drinkers outside, and making of them all, philosophers —

but drink not being his poison, Chad leads on, ignoring the
   importunes of the philosophers, to stay, at least for one pint
   of Les's excellently kept Fuller's —
And under the Lea Bridge (of the Lea Bridge Road) —
crossing now the Lea by the bridge by the weir —
river, rubbish and rats to the right —
high Victorian brick wall to the left, wrought iron gates, more
   wall —
and then round the back —
now on Hackney Marshes, drained, tamed and turned into a
   hundred football pitches by soldiers of the British Army, a
   therapy to debrief and un-excite them, following their victory
   over Jap and German —
a measure to reduce silliness on demob —
and then, Chad and I, breaking in through concrete fencing —
and we're now in the Abandoned Filter Beds —
and let me tell you what these things are:
THEY ARE ENORMOUS SWIMMING BATHS FULL OF
   VEGETATION AND FOLIAGE!

— ? —

I said: 'Chad! How did you know to bring me here?!' —
But he was swinging from trees and gibbering —
he had the gift of tongues now —
he was in the grip of Eospeech.

— ? —

There are six enormous swimming baths —
usually —
sometimes there are seven —
and they were engineered in the 1840s —

London was drinking loads of Lea water and cholera hit big —
and these enormous swimbath things were a system of filtering
   the water —
and they'd been used up till twenty years ago —
and then abandoned —
And Nature had been allowed her reign —
and in one bath she'd ordered a bulrush and reed bed —
in another, high surging marsh grasses surrounding a green
   limpopo lagoon —
another is the sea-side —
but the one down into which I was often to return, is an
   entanglement of luminous green sapling growth and vine —
and down there —
I found it —
(about twenty feet from the wall) —
THE SITE OF THAT DREAM.

— ❓ —

And one time, down there, this thought came:
That dream was long ago —
at the time of that dream this was all under water.

— ❓ —

The Big Case:
The Passive Protagonist is in the Office —
Over the white metal footbridge she comes —
short red skirt —
white top, lacey and laundered —
red high heels —
the very long black hair —
She was originally from Taiwan and her name should've been
   something of a warning:
EMMA MAY WANG.

— ❓ —

The first thing she said: 'I was told I'd find you here in your hat.'

— ② —

The case:
That since 1984 Miss Wang has been writing —
a novel about nurses and songs —
only to find her stuff coming out on the radio, the next day after
    composition —
Is, she wants to know, her phone being bugged? —
'If your phone is being bugged,' I tell her, 'it's as well to know
    this: bugging will make of your receiver, a listening ear at
    ALL times, not just when you're on the phone' —
'Can they read thoughts?' she asked —
'No,' I said, 'I don't think there's a bug invented that can read
    thoughts . . . there might be one which can monitor
    brainwaves but I think all you'd get from that is wavy lines on
    graph paper' —
I hardly think you could deduce a novel about nurses from
    them —
I said it was likely this: that she'd been working hard on a song,
    honing down some line of lyric, and then hears something
    similar on the radio, and thinks: 'Hey! that's mine!' —
She said, No, she didn't think it was that.

— ② —

'Well, maybe you're precognitive, Miss Wang,' I said —
'Maybe you are actually predicting what'll be on tomorrow's
    radio' —
No, she didn't think it was that —
She wondered if it might have something to do with that when

she was made redundant as a nurse, and decided to write
this novel about nursing, that she'd discussed her intention
with a certain Detective Inspector of Longton.

— ❓ —

'Well,' I said, and 'Wow —
and what's this certain Detective Inspector so worried that
    you're going to write? —
so worried that he puts a bug on your phone, night and day, for
    years!? —
What's your picture of this constabulary in Longton? —
shifts of trainee policemen monitoring your bug? —
"Oy!" (guy in headphones) "shut up everyone – she's
    humming!" —
and they crowd round the headset, all these coppers, and they
    get the hang of your latest song —
and sirens blaring they race round to the recording studio —
three hours later it's on wax and *neee-naww! neee-naww!* to the
    local radio station —
and they've got some sinister hold over the Dee-Jay we
    suppose —
"Have this on the air tomorrow, or else, Chum!" —
Ludicrous —
Isn't Longton in the Potteries?' —
Yes, that's right, she lives in Stoke-on-Trent, but this has been
    going on for years and all her friends tell her to give up
    writing, 'cos obviously it's no use if the stuff is going out on
    the radio the next morning —
But I'm not sure, Miss Wang, with your long black hair, that
    your friends have given you the best advice —
put aside your novel, put aside your songs for a bit —
what you're talking to me here and now about —
that is a SUBJECT! —
If you're fantasizing all this, it is still of interest —

if you are precognitive it is very much of interest —
and if anything's going on like you think is going on, just calmly
    assemble the facts, and YOU COULD BE SITTING ON A
    GOLD-MINE.

— ? —

She lived in Stoke-on-Trent, but came to London every ten days
    or so —
and she'd come and see me in the Office —
Half of *Marsh Journal*, Vol II, is devoted to our weird
    conversations —
but I choose not to entertain you with them —
(Just this —
she said one time: 'I bought a guinea pig to love . . . but all it
    did was shit and hide') —
Ah.

— ? —

But she loved those cakes —
George's post-war, noodles of coconut cakes —
she'd eat three at a sitting —
and it was outside George's caff, that she asked: 'Have you got a
    Black and Decker drill?' —
'Yes –' —
With a half inch diameter drill bit?' —
'Possibly –?' —
Could she borrow them? —
What for? —
She had problems . . . with her shelving – what would really be
    best is if I could go back with her to her home in Stoke-on-
    Trent and help her with her shelving –? —
I told her that, no, that wouldn't be possible, and although I put

in all the time I could in the Office, that I was actually very
busy, that I was, myself, in the middle of a script, in fact in
the middle of two, and so the idea of taking time out to go off
with her to Stoke-on-Trent had to be out —
Reluctantly, no, not possible —
And then I heard myself saying: 'Except, maybe, for a couple of
days . . .'

A small frog fell from the sky —
(dropped from the bill of a high-flying goose, I reason) —
landing stunned, on the ground, by our feet —
and I promptly picked up the little creature and threw it in the
    Lea —
I think I regretted the action.

I got off the train at Stoke —
my little bag of tools —
the heavy gloss black hair was on the platform, its weight
    unruffled by the wind —
into a taxi —
It became clear that she thought there were two of us —
that some of the times on the Marsh, she had been interviewed
    by maybe my brother, (I have none), or cousin —
She saw lampposts as sexually depraved Authority figures.*

*'I tell of a woman, who by mental picturings, not only marked the body of her
unborn infant, but transformed herself into the appearance of a tiger, or a
lamppost, or became a weretiger, or a werelamppost—'
                                        Charles Fort, *Wild Talents.*

The layout and furnishings of her small terraced house, were
very similar to those of my parents' old semi-bungalow in
Ilford —
Emma informed me that during her last visit to London she'd
suffered a break-in —
apparently the local constabulary, in league with the BBC and
certain people from Channel 4, had broken in, and inserted
fast-breeding phosphorus machines into the ceilings, and that
there was now a rain of invisible, but deadly particles.

— ? —

She prepared a meal – vegetables in curious batter, and
shrimps, – under a parasol —
and to outwit the BBC and Co., we ate it UNDER THE
TABLE —
and she described how, when alone, she pecked at her meals out
of a drawer —
then she said: 'If your eyes come out, can they be put back?' —
I said that, no, they couldn't —
She said: 'I thought they could –' —
I said: 'Well, no, they can't' —
She got out from under the table; she left the room; and she
came back with a Phrenology Head —
and she asked me to find for her, on her own head, her Area of
Hope —
and I found it for her, tapping on the spot on her skull, relishing
the excuse to feel her hair —
'People's heads don't ever just fall off, do they. . . ?' she said —
I told her they didn't —
and she sought my opinion on St Phyllis, evidently a Catholic
Martyr, who, upon decapitation, had picked up her head and
kissed it —
and I said: 'Could we get on with the shelves now?'

— ? —

But not quite yet, apparently —
something that could only be done by one needed preparing
    first —
the shelving problem was in her upstairs —
and she took my tool bag —
I was bade stay down in the dining parlour —·
I was looking around to see how I might pass my time till I was
    summoned —
'Hey!' I called up to her, 'Where's your radio? and TV?' —
She had thrown them out because —
THEY HAD STARTED TO ADDRESS HER DIRECTLY.

— ? —

I sat for a short while —
I began to see specks in the air —
but these were presumably not phosphorus particles, as those, I
    had been informed, were invisible —
and then I began to poke about through her things.

— ? —

And one drawer was full of feathers —
and in another drawer I found large format photos of beaches —
(some were maybe deserts) —
and on many of the photos was writing —
in silver ink —
I guess lines from her lyrics —
'Oh, when's the time for coming home?' —
and 'The years fly by like fruit gums' —
and 'In May I wear my Orange Coat' —
and I was now hearing the buzz of the drill from upstairs —

I supposed I ought to go up and help —
but I'd just seen, in a corner, what looked like a two-foot high
    wooden feather —
I investigated, and, no, not a feather, an erotic statuette, turned
    modestly to the wall:
a red man, crouching in green trousers, and reaching up,
    literally, into the nethers of a long black-haired goddess, left
    knee raised high —
and the drilling had stopped —
and then I saw that Emma May Wang was at the foot of the
    stairs —
and she was smiling, uncharacteristically, beautifully,
    CHIRPILY —
LIKE A YOUNG GIRL, WHO'S JUST SCORED A GOAL
    AT A HOCKEY MATCH.

And then I was conscious of a strange smell —
what's that smell? —
and then I realized —
Oh yes! —
(oh blimey) —
I WAS EXUDING THE STICKY OF CHILDHOOD.

And love is now being made —
foot of the stairs, standing position —
and, black hair of the goddess —
this is probably the sublimest moment, so far, of your tacky life,
    Campbell —
but might it not even be topped? —
if we could shift the proceedings onto the sofa over there? —

that sofa, so like my old Mum and Dad's . . .
and then I was aware that I was looking at blood.

— ? —

And coming out of the blood was wire —
a round hole of pulsing blood in her head —
she'd trepanned herself with the Black and Decker —
made a hole in her Hope —
(been fixing her own shelving) —
But what to make of the wire . . .
I said: 'You just sit down there – You've had a bit of an
     accident – Don't touch your head –' —
looking up the directory for the hospital number —
(What is that wire. . . ? —
Like some awful AERIAL —
Has she been so missing her radio that she's making an
     experiment in Direct Reception. . . ? —
Looking at the wire made my teeth go funny) —
Through to the hospital —
They're only sending out ambulances on emergencies —
I said: 'Well this is a lady who's just bored a hole in her
     head –' —
'Can she walk?' —
I said, 'I dunno –' —
'Well, see if she can walk –' —
(the hospital was just up the hill, she said) —
I tried a taxi firm but they'd got no taxis —
well, let's see if she can walk . . .
yes, she's fine, she's happy to walk —
and I tidied her up —
and holding her gently but firmly —
(I didn't want to spill her) —
we set off into the night.

— ? —

And it was one of those nights when you hear a lot of wind, but
    you don't feel any —
and as we rounded the corner, and only up the hill to go —
my shoes —
I had these heavy black shoes on —
and I was worried, holding her tight and steady, that the click of
    the heels might jolt her —
so I took them off and put them over a hedge into someone's
    garden —
and as we passed the church, I was surprised, given the lateness
    of the hour, to hear a congregation lustily singing a hymn —
but then the hymn STUCK —
and restarted a few phrases back —
and I thought: That's no congregation in there —
it's a lonely vicar playing his records —
and I give that as the moment that I realized I had fallen in love
    with Emma May Wang —
and I was OK about the aerial —
and it wasn't an aerial, it was a feather —
its plumes and barbs blown on the wind.

— ? —

Through the imposing gates of the Infirmary —
up an avenue of trees —
my arm around her —
a couple of some style —
Doors, more like those of a fine old hotel, are opened for us —
and a red carpet! —
and of a rich pile, I can attest, through my socks.

— ? —

And she is seen commendably quickly —
and she'd said no word from the bottom of her stairs till now —
but now, with the handsome young doctor, she is speaking
   lucidly:
You see, she'd had this feeling, this thought, well not a thought,
   more a feeling, that she hadn't got any brain, and it had kept
   bothering her, this doubt, so she'd thought well let's get this
   worry out of the way, and so she'd bored the hole in her head,
   and felt in with coat-hanger wire, and she was so pleased to
   find that, yes, there was a load of stuff in there, and so happy
   that she was now with someone who knew what he was doing
   who could get it out for her, because you never knew the sort
   of damage you might do, playing about like this, did you.

— ? —

Three weeks later I was talking to a Medical Philosopher outside
   the Anchor and Hope —
he knew Emma a bit —
'Where exactly did she do it?' —
'Right here,' I said, indicating my Area of Hope —
'Wow!' he said, 'well, she got it right – not so many years ago,
   when they used to do that operation a lot, actually they got a
   lot of success with it – she could have done herself a favour
   there, her – the mistake was the coat-hanger wire.'

— ? —

I had to stay more than the 'couple of days' in Stoke —
and in the crematorium chapel —
three neighbours, and Gent in Raincoat —
(the certain Detective Inspector from Longton?) —
organ —
and then Frank Bailey, nice man, the Funeral Director, beside
   me —

and he passes me a plastic bag —
and in it —
I'd asked Frank if I could be allowed a lock of Emma's hair —
here, in the bag, was the entire mane —
and the organ swells —
jubilantly —
doors open themselves —
we see the gas jets —
and the coffin is conveyed by a roller system towards the
    flames —
the doors tastefully closing themselves before its journey's end.

— ? —

And no-one to stop me and I took the statuette —
and on the train back to London, the Black and Decker in my
    tool-bag with the hair, and the erotic statuette —
and my hands reached into the bag and they felt the hair —
and they brought out the statuette —
and it didn't seem at all the thing to be seen with on a British
    train, so I kept it under the table —
but handling the rampant totem, I may have come close to
    comprehending what had REALLY taken me to Stoke —
something like this?:
that I had been seeking my redemption through a Red Indian
    Phantasm Lady —
but as to whether, by her brief and curious incarnation I had
    gained it —
that was severely open to doubt.

— ? —

THREE

And back home now —
and outside George's caff —
and eating (deliberately) a post-war noodle cake —
staring into the oily murk of the Lea —
thoughts and memories (and regrets) —
slow-flowing —
merging —
and off to the pub —
Opening Time to well past Drink Up, with the Philosophers,
    outside the Anchor and Hope, chummy, huddled, in an early
    snow-fall —
and on the stagger home, passing the riverside flats of
    Watermint Quay, in the lock-up for the residents' dustbins,
    the lock broken, and intending to winter in there:
CHAD.

— ❓ —

But Chad now, sadly, mutated into his own Mother —
wrapped in a lady's coat which was on the turn from green to
    brown —
(or vice-versa) —
and saying over: 'Oh look at his shoes! Will you look at my
    boy's shoes! The state of them!' —
and, indeed, there wasn't much left of his shoes —

and I said: 'Don't worry about your shoes, Chad – I'll sort your
   shoes out – just hang on here –' —
and I nipped off home —
my intention to bring him a tenner —
he could go to the Spastics shop in the morning, and get himself
   shod for ten quid —
(probably have a bit over for a jersey) —
but I found myself going back with £200 —
Chad muttering into his plastic bag —
I showed Chad the notes —
made him aware of the enormous amount —
and as I gave him the money I took from him his plastic bag of
   substance —
'But that's for this,' I said, 'and I don't mean just this bag – for
   ever – no more bags – do you understand?' —
and I think he did —
he felt around in one of the bins and produced a miniature oil
   painting —
flowers in a blue vase —
and he gave it to me —
and then, before his gaze, I threw his bag of substance into the
   Lea.

And I went home, and couldn't reason with why I didn't feel
   better about the transaction —
I'd given him 200 quid —
I'd taken his substance from him —
(I'd taken his substance from him) —
I'D TAKEN HIS SUBSTANCE FROM HIM! —
O shit! —
That suddenly had a dark ring —
I ran back down to the bins —
He wasn't there —

I spent the whole of the next day in the Office —
He didn't show up —
Or the next day —
I never saw him again —
(except I fear I may.)

— ? —

Outside George's caff —
Captain Ken Kelly eating an egg, and dredging up memories of
    Dotty the water-tart —
and suddenly I said: 'There's a body going by!' —
George came out, and we looked in the river —
and it might be a body —
if it was floating by arse up —
we watched the thing pass slowly under the bridge —
perhaps it wasn't a body —
and back to Dotty and the Brothel Boat Era when everything
    round here was fucking terrific.

— ? —

But a couple of days later George said to me:
'You were right – it was a body – they fished it out at Old Ford
    Lock –' —
I said: 'What happens to a body after it's fished out at Old Ford
    Lock?' —
George said: 'It'd go to Hackney Mortuary.'

— ? —

'How well did you know your missing person?' said the man at
    Hackney Mortuary —

I said I'd met him on several occasions —
'So you didn't know him well enough to make a positive
 identification with the body alone?' —
(What does he mean? —
He's going to come with me and pull out the drawer, isn't
 he?) —
What he meant was without the head —
I said: 'What's happened to the head?' —
He said: 'It's gone to Farringdon –' —
I said: 'Why?' —
He said: 'It happens. I'll give you the address if you like.'

Farringdon —
N. Evans Associates and I was in luck —
they were closed —
perhaps they were taking an early lunch —
maybe they get all the heads sorted by Wednesday —
Anyway, I thought, sod it, had enough, going home.

Platform Farringdon Tube Station deserted —
then enter two roaring men —
lurching, rolling and both called Jimmy —
I took up a bizarrely unalarming posture by the chocolate
 machine —
I by-passed the musculature of Jimmy One's eyeballs, but failed
 with Jimmy Two's —
I turned slowly from the chocolate machine and was faced with
 SEETHE —
a squat, hideous man built like half a dozen shit-houses —
WRATH —

So filled with wrath he couldn't speak —
coming from his mouth and nose a disgusting foam —
but then, through the nauseous froth, came words, and they
    were these:
'I'M GOING TO THROW YOU ON THE LINES!' —
I said, 'Why?'
He said: 'YOU KNOW WHY!!' —
I said: 'Well, I'm sorry, I don't –' —
Froth, foam, then:
'BECAUSE I'M POTTY AND I'M GOING TO DRIVE YOU
    POTTY AND THEN I'M GOING TO THROW YOU ON
    THE LINES!' —
The train comes in —
I dodge him —
I'm on the tube —
but so is he —
in pursuit —
Tube starting off —
and he's pursuing me up the carriage —
I have to go through the emergency door into the next
    carriage —
he's through it too —
falling on people, roaring, but keeping up —
and King's Cross and I'm out and escaped.

But I hadn't escaped damage from the encounter —
it was my neck —
I'd lost the lubrication of the neck vertebrae —
or maybe it was psychological —
and that I was scrunching down my head —
so as to be sure it was still there.

Whichever the cause, it was a depressing state —
and come the Saturday I knew I must take the cheering up of
    myself in hand —
I decided to go to Dingwall's Market at Camden Lock —
(memories of great times in that place) —
but I wasn't prepared for how popular it's become —
and the noise and the throng and my neck —
it was too much effort to fight through to a favourite stall:
The Stall of Wooden Ties —
they look like regular ties —
could be mistaken for suede —
hand-carved by P.C. Slade, the whittling constable of Crediton,
    Devon —
but, as I say, I'd passed it by —
but the carving copper caught up with me —
he showed me his new line:
'With Designer Woodworm' —
and he put his latest model on me —
(a ribbon Velcros round the neck) —
and he wanted no money for it —
he'd seen me in something on the telly and assumed I now
    mixed with important people —
'You'll wear it?' he said —
'Yes,' I said —
he battled back to his stall —
and wood tie around my creaky neck —
I felt like a fully paid up member of the Dick Society.

I'd now got round to the back of the market —
behind the Le Routier Restaurant (pricey but good) —
and was resting amongst the splendid absence of happy people
    by the canal lock —
could just see the last market stall through the trellis —

an Objet de Crap stall —
and then I was aware that I was not alone —
a man probably in his mid-twenties —
good-looking in a way —
a cut down white shirt and tight black trousers —
the sort of job you'd play Hamlet in —
and he said: 'Have you ever been in love?' —
I said: '. . . Yes –' —
and he said: 'Have you ever fallen in love suddenly, with such
    an intensity, that you knew you had to possess that
    person?' —
I said: '. . . Something like that . . . possibly . . . yes –' —
He said: 'I'm Noddy –' —
and he held out a large hand —
and I gave him mine —
and squeezing it into pain, smiling, he said: 'What's your
    name?' —
'Ken –' —
He said: 'Why aren't you talking to me, Kenneth?' DID YOU
    THINK YOU'D FOUND A SAFE PLACE AT LAST?' —
I said: 'Why did you squeeze my hand so hard?' —
He said: 'Because I wanted you to feel my skin; my flesh – I
    would like you to feel my heart –' —
and he took my hand and put it inside his shirt —
and he said: 'It's pumping very hard, isn't it; very fast. . . ?' —
'Yes it is –' —
'But it's not love though – that's the unfortunate part, Kenneth –
    it's hate – the real thing – Here's how it'll go:
we'll just hang around here until whatever it is wells up inside
    me and whatever has to be done will do itself —
I am merely to be the agency.'

— ❓ —

I have done a course on How to be a More Remarkable
    Person —

and one of the tips we got was:
If you encounter a dangerous customer you should note which is
    the weaker side of the face, and you should look, without
    deviation, into the eye of the weaker side —
and this, I had been doing for some time, with Noddy.

— ❓ —

But, looking intently at one point, one still retains a
    considerable peripheral vision —
and I had been hoping to see a friend turn up in it —
and then just anybody —
but so far no-one —
I was aware only of what I'd taken to be a cloth mushroom,
    which I could see through the trellis, hanging from the awning
    of the Objet de Crap stall —
and at this moment it was caught in the breeze and it turned
    round and I saw that it wasn't a cloth mushroom, it was a doll,
    a little oriental doll lady, and I thought:
so this is my only Area of Hope —
that Miss Emma May Wang is right now interceding for me on
    some other plane —
and Noddy is saying: 'You put people into compartments don't
    you?' —
and I said: '. . . Sometimes –' —
'Which of your compartments are you putting me in?' —
I said: 'I don't have one ready for you yet –' —
and he said: 'Are you acquainted with the music of Wagner?' —
and suddenly my head was a riot in a telephone exchange but
    from somewhere way at the back of the mayhem was someone
    jumping, shouting, determined that through the confusion his
    message would get through, and it was Prettyboy Tentringer
    and he was shouting and he was shouting and I couldn't hear
    through the noise of the Pandemonium and then I heard and
    then I heard and what he was saying was:

'SPEAR HIM!' —
and I ripped off my tie and speared the awful fellow into the
canal.

— ? —

And when I got home I thought: 'I think I better get out of
London –' —
I know, go and visit my friends in Liverpool —
I pack a few things —
Euston Station —
in line for my ticket, and I think, no, I can't go to Liverpool
because the train stops at STOKE-ON-TRENT —
and then I think, I know, I'll go to Paddington Station —
I couldn't think what all places you might go to from Paddington
Station —
and I thought, well, if I don't know where I'm going nor will
anyone else.

— ? —

And so now coming up from the Tube onto Paddington Station
Main Line —
passing the statue of Isambard Kingdom Brunel, seated, and
looking askance, it seems, at our latest engineering feat —
the nine-seater plastic pod arrangement —
so that nine people may sit on the same seat with minimum
chance of meeting —
circular pods —
I sat on a pod to study the Menu of Possibilities —
and then happening to glance at the Taxi queue just past
Platform 8 —
heading the queue was ANDY JONES! —
ANDEE! —

But by the time I got there he'd disappeared —
(into a taxi I suppose) —
but coming back from the rank I am passing between the cars
   parked slantwise towards the exit slip road and it seems to me
   that I am passing my old mauve Marina —
what was its registration? —
can't remember —
but I note the keys have been left in the ignition —
and I return to my pod —
and I read through the list of places served from Paddington —
I read through the list three times —
and I find it very depressing reading —
many places —
but really no place to go.

— ❓ —

'He went for an ice-cream at the interval' —
'He went around the horses' —
He went to Paddington Station —
what was this (vision?) of Andy Jones? —
to disappear? —
vanish? —
teleport off? —
and I fancied I knew how it might be accomplished —
comes into my mind the opening page of *LO!*:
'A naked man in a city street HYPHEN the track of a horse in
   volcanic mud HYPHEN the mystery of reindeer's ears
   HYPHEN' —
and the hyphens (—) were beginning to lift off the page —
'an appalling cherub appears in the sea HYPHEN' —
and now the hyphen is beginning to turn towards me —
and when it points directly at me —
that's when I'll go! —
'Showers of frogs and blizzards of snails' —

HYPHEN almost at me now —
and then the Voice is shrieking: 'Don't you think there are one
   or two items you should pay for before you leave?' —
I said: 'Lord, what do you mean? You mean there IS a Hell?' —
'Yes, it's for those who've ever thought there was one –' —
'And it's bad is it?' —
'It's as bad as you've ever thought it was –' —
I was thinking, up past your ears in bubbling shit and a duff
   snorkel —
'Don't be optimistic,' said the Voice.

— ? —

And the Voice said: 'Would you like me to organize a
   punishment for you here?' —
I said: 'Like what?' —
and the Voice said: 'Well you know that car you saw with the
   key in the ignition? —
go and steal it –' —
I thought and I said No —
I said: 'No, I don't want to do that –' —
and the Voice said: 'That's how come it would have been a
   punishment –' —
I was beginning to get a handle on the concept —
and then the Voice came up with another suggestion: 'Take your
   little bag of belongings and go down into the Gentlemen's
   Convenience –' —
(I looked to see where this was – beyond Platform 1) —
'Go into whichever cubicle seems to summon you, put your bag
   on the lavatory seat, take off all your clothes, and pile them
   up on top of the bag, and set light to it all in three places —
AND THEN STEAL THE MARINA!' —
I said: 'And then I'll be happy?' —
The Voice said: 'I think there's a chance –' —
I said: 'Are you inside me or outside me?' —

and the Voice said: 'I'm not going to tell you –' —
And then the Voice said: 'I'll tell you if you do it.'

— ❓ —

And that's how come I'm going passed the Bureau de Change
  and the Croissant Shop, and turning right beside Platform 1,
  and towards the Gentlemen's Convenience, just by the Tie
  Rack —
and parked outside is an Electric Courtesy Vehicle, with driver,
  and passed them and down into the Gents —
and down there it is RED —
the ceilings are red —
the floor is red —
the cubicles are red —
and I'm now in one —
did it 'summon' me? —
I don't know —
maybe it did:
beside the WC pedestal is a pair of black shoes in good nick —
and they worry me, the shoes —
and I've taken all my clothes off —
they're in a pile, on my bag, on the lav seat —
but the shoes? —
are the shoes to be part of my pyrotechnic revel? —
No —
There was no mention of shoes —
they're innocent, bystander shoes —
and I set light to it all in three places —
deliberately firing the crutch of my trousers with the first
  match —
but I don't go —
and I don't know why —
it's gone from smouldering into burning —

and then my hand reaches through the flames and pulls from the
   bag —
EMMA'S HAIR.

— ❓ —

And with Emma's hair in my hand, I'm ok, and I'm out of the
   cubicle, and I'll tell you something peculiar about the
   Paddington Gents —
the cubicles are NUMBERED! —
I thought, what are they numbered for? —
Are we on TV? —
('Come out Number 9—your hour is up!—') —
and now passing a couple of guys having a piddle, and they
   don't see me, and up the stairs, and the Courtesy Vehicle is
   still there, but the driver has gone —
and then a middle-aged Hasidic gentleman —
I strike a bizarrely un-alarming pose —
AND HE DOESN'T SEE ME! —
and the folk at Menzie's haven't seen me —
and I'm now behind the Bureau de Change and the Croissant
   Shop —
at the Platform heads —
and creeping past a mother and daughter —
they don't see me because they're studying Arrival Times on a
   Video Monitor, Platform 2 —
But then —
coming down the alley to Platforms 3/4, two middle aged ladies,
   and a young man in ludicrously coloured shorts —
they have seen me —
and breaking into a run —
and a *Poop*! from behind me —
the Electric Courtesy Vehicle in pathetic pursuit —
(hey, my neck's ok!) —
but, now the alley which comes down to Platforms 5/6 —

Seen by a big, black British Rail Official —
and he's blowing his WHISTLE —
and seen by the Pod People —
and they're turning to each other —
My God, I've united the Pod People! —
(running flat out now) —
and the Taxi queue is EXCITED —
and coming down from the slip road a Royal Mail Van —
and the larger sort of postman getting out —
hue and cry! —
and it seems that everyone thinks that I'm making for the Taxi
    queue —
and I keep up this pretence —
and then when I get past Platform 8, I turn —
Now heading towards the Marina —
and I think I can make it —
AND THEN I PRAY —
(and let me tell you something about REAL prayer: it is
    LIQUID in form —
it comes squirting out of every pore) —
and this is my prayer:
'Let that not be my old Marina!' —
(that thing never started first time!) —
and I'm going to make it! —
and I'm in the car —
about to start it —
and then I remember that I've got a deal riding on this —
and I say: 'So are you INSIDE me or OUTSIDE me?' —
and the Voice says: 'You're inside ME.'

— ❓ —

And I couldn't get the picture of that —
and that was my undoing —
car door flung open —

and I am flown from the car as if in a ballet —
and as I'm flown I'm able to see smoke gloriously issuing from
   the Gents on Platform 1 —
Fort said: 'An unclothed man shocks a crowd – a moment later,
   if nobody is generous with an overcoat, somebody is collecting
   handkerchiefs to knot around him –' —
that's how it was in the thirties —
(when the Brothel Fleet steamed the Lea) —
but things have changed —
they're quite violent now —
or maybe it was something about me? —
Emma's HAIR? —
they're hitting me into a mail-bag —
and the last thing I see is 'TRAVELLER'S REST' —
and then the RAMP which comes down onto the far end of the
   station.

and then I was no longer on paddington station I was in
the swimming bath of veg and foliage at the appointed
spot and there was the geezer ten feet away and he had
his back to me and he was planting flowers and playing
golf and jerking off all in the same moment and I knew I
must get round there and meet him but I could only walk
in an agonizingly slow careful mince and I noted my
elbow was professionally bandaged perhaps I'd just had
an arsehole graft and now I've made it I've minced
round and I'm meeting the geezer and the large bulgy
eyes bring to mind andy jones but then the many arms
make me think of the prophet but most it's the frog from
the lino kissed into princehood and it's not he's speaking
it is that I am receiving from him and this is what I'm
receiving in my o-oringy coat in my o-oringy coat in my
o-oringy coat and was he wearing an orange coat no he

wasn't in my o-oringy coat constantly repeated and it was
doing something to me or undoing something in me in
my o-oringy coat as if all my life has been a wilful act of
forgetting in my o-oringy coat and I feel something
loosening in my o-oringy coat and suddenly whoop a trap
door at the back of my head has opened and another
trap door whoop at the front and I am hurtling
backwards and forwards through time at the same time
backwards past lives flying by like fruit gums I am now
way back I am something examining primordial ice an
onion and a lump of ice and what have they in common I
am looking at botanical forms in the first ice and I can
predict jungles and forwards I have gone so far forwards
yes these are machines and still in a sense enquiring on
but in a finitely cold system whose sun has died in my o-
oringy coat and turning round holding hand number
three of the many armed andy jones frog prophet miss
nscho-tchi wang all put back together and resplendently
adorned in a whole draw load of feathers in my o-oringy
coat and chad lurking in the luminous green young
sapling growth but no bag no bag no need of bag now in
my o-oringy coat in my o-oringy coat and they're trying
to get me to look at something the stones hey the stones
are shifting and moving and o wow and o wow non-
physical entities in a flash manifesting with sniggering
faces and exquisite wings in my o-oringy coat in my o-
oringy coat and then I see it yes I see it the thread of
marching time and I see the actual thread in my o-oringy
coat the thread and coming out from under a table young
mum and young dad and I know who that is it must be
time to perform and I stretch out a hand but not a hand I
recognize perhaps it's tentringer's hand and I touch time
I touch the thread of marching time I twang it listen the
thread of marching time is elastic in my o-oringy coat
I've got it this is the job here's the commission
YOU'VE GOT TO GET HOLD OF THE THREAD OF

MARCHING TIME AND PULL THE FUCK
THING DOWN AND GET ON IT AND PANG
YOURSELF TO THE INFINITUDE OF ABSOLUTE
MIND.

Pigspurt
– or Six Pigs from Happiness

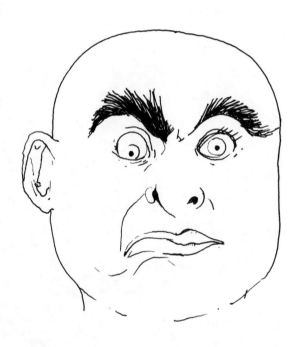

'Like Stanislavsky and Brecht, I've invented an entirely new method of acting, I call it the *enantiodromic approach*. The theory of enantiodromia is that the left and right sides of your face represent different personalities. If you're clever with mirrors you'll see what I mean. My right side, for instance, is that of an inept housewife and the left side – or "facet" as we call it – is that of a spanking squire!'

Ken Campbell

Written and performed by Ken Campbell, *Pigspurt* was premièred at the Riverside Studios, London and transferred to the Almeida Theatre, London in 1992 before embarking on a tour of the UK, Amsterdam and, in 1993, Australia and the Royal National Theatre, London. It won a *Time Out* Award in 1992.

Pigspurt theme and incidental music by Richard Kilgour

'**** Nose' by Buster Bloodvessel (Bad Manners)

Paintings and props by Mitch Davies

Produced by Colin Watkeys

'He's all right. He's all right' —
People are always coming up to me and saying 'How's Alf?'
    because they recognize me from the *In Sickness and in Health*
    thing —
They don't know my name, they don't know my character's
    name and so they say:
'How's Alf?' —
And I say: 'He's all right' —
Sometimes they pop up from holes in the road: 'How's Alf?'
    'He's all right' —
They break ranks from National Front marches: 'How's Alf?'
    Fuck off. 'He's all right.'

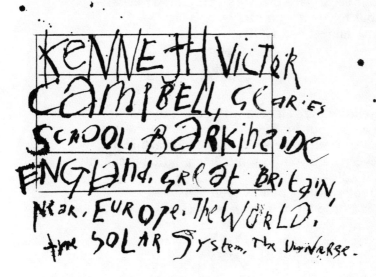

That's the style of thing we used to write on our exercise
   books when we were six and three-quarters —
in case the things got lost in space.

My first brush with show business was at Gearies School —
Showtime on Friday afternoons —
Being born in the war we didn't have many toys —
And so the form was if you'd got a toy no one had seen yet,
   you'd bring it along on a Friday afternoon and show it to the
   other kids.

But one afternoon our Showtime was cancelled —
And our class (we were Miss O'Halloran's class) —
were put together with Mrs Denn's class —
And the subject was GOD.

Apparently we are all born with a bit of the Almighty inside us —
we've all got our bit of God —
and it's situated somewhere in the stomach region —
And every time you do something a little bit naughty —
like tell a lie —
(apparently writing a lie is even worse) —
you get a little bit of *dirty in your God*.

Did you know that recently there'd been chaps applying for
    entry Up There —
and their Gods *had been filthy*? —
There'd been cases of fellows whose Gods had been completely
    eaten away —
'Yes, Janet?' (A question from Janet Dean at the back) —
'Do you mean Germans, Miss O'Halloran?' —
'Yes, Janet, very good' —
Lately, people who'd been applying for entrance Up There
    with totally eaten away Gods had been Germans —
And also Japanese —
Listen! Mrs Denn is going to be most upset *indeed* if any of
    our year are caught applying for entrance Up There with
    completely eaten away Gods.

And now, to help us with the concept —
we're only six and three-quarters —
some of us are only six-and-a-half! —
are handed round autopsy liver photographs —
First the photo of the liver of a terminal alcoholic —
which we have to compare with the fine frisky liver of a healthy-
    living sort of chap —
(Really a quite striking afternoon) —
'Yes? Yes, Janet?' —
Janet wants to know, is there any way you can clean up your
    God —
'Yes Janet, we're glad you asked that, of course there is —
of course there's a way you can clean up your God' —
What you've got to do: you've got to do two good things
    for every one bad thing —
Two to one is the ratio.

Also slippering —
Slippering will help —
Having the backs of your legs (Miss O'Halloran) or your bottom
    (Mrs Denn) bashed at with a shoe —
that'll get it down a bit —
But you're still going to have to do one good thing —
'Yes Peter?' —
A question from Peter Sarbutt —
Peter wants to know, can you meet God without dying? —
'Yes, Peter, you can. But it will be *in the most unlikely place*' —
This gives rise to a lot of conjecture in the playground —
as to where that might be —
we can think up some very unlikely places! —
But no!! —
If you can *think* of it, it won't be it!!! —
It'll be *even more unlikely than that*!!!!

Every morning you've got to write up your diary —
Even if nothing's happened to you —
you've still got to write about it —
you've got to put it in your diary —
But if anything a wee bit sensational has happened to you —
maybe you'll have the honour of reading out your diary to
    Miss O'Halloran and the class —
And I used to like to go for that honour —
But very often this would mean *lying in my diary*.

So a dubious glory —
but as I go back to my desk —
I can feel the dirtiness gnawing into my God.

But I manage to get hold of Him —
got Him on the direct line —
'It's alright actually sir, all this lying I've been doing in my
    diary because I won't ever be doing that again, lying in my
    diary, and anyway I'll be doing two good things for it, and
    two good things for yesterday's one as well . . .' —
Maybe I ought to make a full confession of everything —
request a programme of slippering from Mrs Denn and Miss
    O'Halloran —
Get the odds in my favour —
(Mind, it didn't sound too great Up There —
all that hymn singing —
But I'd enjoy the flying —
and definitely to be preferred to the alternative as outlined
    by Mrs Denn.)

I wrote a little poem at this time which went:

'My diary is a liary
A diary of lies
My God-all-dirty diary
In heaven for me no pies' —

And even to this day, if I repeat over and over again:
'No pies . . . *No pies* . . . There's going to be NO PIES for
    you, Kenneth!'
Tears stream down my face.

About six months after Dirtying-up-your-God-Friday a new boy
    was put into the school and he was put into the desk next to
    mine —
and we became best friends —
His name was Derek —
and one playtime I unburdened myself on Derek as to all
    this lying I'd been doing in my diary —
But Derek said:
(but Derek had not had the benefit of autopsy liver photographs)
'Not to worry, because there's *no such thing as God* —
and anyway He's stupid.' —
Sometimes I felt that Derek had maybe three-quarters convinced
    me —
Sometimes I could be almost as happy and breezy as Derek.

Sad to relate, when Derek was eleven, his mother (a devout
    Methodist) chopped him to bits —
Some of the bits weren't found —
And the *Ilford Recorder* which covered all the sensational aspects
    of the case in every detail, didn't tell us —
maybe they didn't know —
whether or not this was down to a *theological altercation*.

'For you Carstairs, it is the —' —
I am attempting an impression of the late Stuart Pearce —
When I left the Royal Academy of Dramatic Art in 1960, after
 a lot of letters they eventually let me in at the Colchester
 Repertattery Company —
a weekly Rep establishment —
and undoubtedly the God there was Stuart Pearce.
Stuart Pearce was probably the last in that great line of 'actor-
 laddies' —
This means that, equipped with a silver-topped cane, you greet
 younger members of the Co, like myself, with *'Hello, dear
 boy!'* —
Stuart had toured in the war years with the Tod Slaughter
 Melodrama Company —
and he styled himself *'eccentric character actor'* —
And this means that you deliver your many and varied
 performances *through your nose* —
For Stuart Pearce it was like his piercer was his nose —
an extraordinary prying, enquiring, prodding, poking organ —
Indeed it was Stuart's pride that by the Friday —
(these shows only lasted a week) —
that by the Friday, Stuart would have contrived to be touching
 his nose upon the nose of a fellow actor —
(Dramatically justified, in a sense, by Stuart's baroque, heavily
 ornamented performance style —)
Which of course led to a lot of tension if you were on stage
 with Stuart in the early part of the week —
when the nose was seeking out its Friday quarry.

Sensational he was on the Friday of some
    thriller —
Goes Stuart: '*A knife in the back . . . is not what we call
    . . . a normal death, CARSTAIRS!*' —
Stuart's piercer-nose narrowly missing the Carstairs hooter but
    catching him on the cheek —
and cutting it! —
He'd sliced Carstairs' cheek with his nose! —
continuing: – '*For you Carstairs, it is the* —' —
and he spells it out with his now crimson-tipped nose:

'*e ... n ... d ...*' –

How had Stuart done it? —
How had he cut Carstairs with his nose? —
Various theories . . .
some said that Stuart must have glued up his nose a shard
    of razor blade —
others said he had simply crushed a blood capsule in his nostril
    and snotted it at Carstairs.

When Stuart left Colchester to go off to finer things with
the Penguin Players, the place was a bit desolate —
But then, at Christmas: the panto —
and we had Hugh Hastings playing the piano —
And Hugh Hastings was a name in those days —
Hugh Hastings had written a naval comedy —
It had been on in the West End: *Seagulls Over Sorrento* —
But by this time nobody much was doing it —
it was just being done in prisons —
and Hugh Hastings was reduced to playing the piano for the
    Colchester Repertattery panto —

Anyway, I was having a drink with Hugh in the pub one
   lunchtime and Hugh started talking about his acting career —
Well actually I hadn't known he'd got one —
A multi-talent: writing naval comedies, playing the piano . . .
   and now an acting career —
But this was the extraordinary thing: Hugh Hastings was only
   interested in playing Third Act Detective Inspectors in
   thrillers —
THIRD ACT DETECTIVE INSPECTORS!? —
they're the sort of part you get lumbered with, aren't they? —
hardly, surely, a career goal? —
'Oh no no no!' —
Not according to Hugh —
'No!' he said. 'No' —
He said: 'The Third Act Detective Inspector is the nearest
   thing we have today to the fine old tradition of *deus ex
   machina*!' —
What's that!? —
Well, in order to understand *deus ex machina* you've got to
   go back in time —
Evidently the ancient Greeks, Sophocles and Co, if they'd've
   got their plots to such a pass that they couldn't logically
   resolve them —
it would be time then to call down the *deus ex machina* —
The *deus* being the god, and the *machina* this bunch of cogs
   and rope and wotnot —
And the god comes clanking down —
and with his deific powers he'd be able to put things in harmony
   again —
And Hugh said: 'Isn't that the same as your Third Act Detective
   Inspector? —
You've got two-and-a-half acts of human beings fucking up,
   and then, Whoomph! —
The Inspector calls! —
And with his metropolitan magic he puts things back in order?
'No, no,' said Hugh, 'a Third Act Detective Inspector —

Man, it's a *theophany*.* —
With a Third Act Detective Inspector you can romp away
   with the thunder with the GLORY of any thriller —
if you know the secret' —
'Well,' I said. 'Here's another half, Hugh —
A secret? You mean there's a secret to playing Third Act
   Detective Inspectors?' —
'Mmm,' he said, 'oh yes —
first of all, you've got to learn the lines' —
And that was revolutionary talk in those days —
Learn the lines? —
you always played a Third Act Detective Inspector with a
   notebook —
you'd got all your lines written in the notebook —
(poised as if to write answer – in fact reading line: —
'*And where were you on the night of the fourteenth*?') —
Hugh said, 'Don't even *have* a notebook —
And then,' he said (and this is the big one) —
'*look for clues.*' —
Wow —
'*Where were you . . .* (looking under hat) —
on the night of er . . . (finding sausage) —
the fourteenth? . . .' (examining sausage with magnifying glass) —
Wow —

And now life is minutes on a clock until I get a Third Act
   Detective Inspector —
and sooner or later, I thought, I gotta get one —
and it was later —
The drama to be *Signpost to Murder* by Monte Doyle —

Theophany: n., pl. -ies. A manifestation of a deity to a man in a form that, though visible,
is not necessarily material. [*Chambers Dictionary*]

me to play Inspector Bickford, coming on (classically) halfway
  through Act Three —
We had a new leading man that week, a fellow called Ted
  Webster —
the lead part being a lunatic —
a very dangerous lunatic escaped from the lunatic asylum —
He bursts in on a lone woman in a country house —
he begins to molest, to maraud her —
Then, towards the end of Act Two —
it begins to transpire that —
just possibly —
she's ghastlier, she's pottier than he is! Ha Ha! —
But then . . . —
Well, I'm not going to spoil it for you —
If David Hare's suddenly running out of steam
they may be wanting to mount a Monte Doyle revival season.

Anyway, for a Third Act Detective Inspector at Colchester
  in 1960, you only had two mornings' rehearsal —
The first rehearsal: director Bernard Kelly looks up over his
  half-glasses and says, 'You're not using a notebook, Ken?' —
I said, 'No Bernard, I thought I'd learn the lines.' —
'Learn the lines!' —
company exchanging 'Whoops ducky!' looks —
Since merely learning the lines so phased everyone, I thought
  I'd better not look for clues at the rehearsal —
I didn't want to get that cut —
But I was looking around for the sort of places you might
  look for clues come the opening night —
Indeed I had a scheme developing to secrete sundry clues
  in and under things, both meaningful and red-herring.

Opening night Monday, and the first two-and-a-half acts had
     gone what Ted Webster and Margaret Thing, the leading
     lady, would have called 'well' —
By 'well' they'd've meant that there'd not been a chuckle —
not a titter from the house —
Therefore the good people of Colchester must have been utterly
     captivated by Monte Doyle's desperate plotting —
Then: Enter Inspector Bickford —
And I start looking for clues —
And wow! —
The whole place went up! —
A gale of laughter – Force 10! —
And the Bishop of Colchester in the front row, and he's going,
     'UH HAHH! HA-HAHHH!! UH HA!!! HA-HAHHH!!!!' —
I thought, I must remember to write a thank-you letter to
     Hugh, tell him how well it's gone —
And then at the bowing, thunderous applause —
And I thought, probably two-thirds of it is down to me —
But a few minutes later —
the metal door of my changing-hutch is burst rudely open —
And there was Ted Webster —
he'd put on a kilt for this occasion —
and he took the fire bucket off the wall —
full of old greasy water been there thirty years —
and he slung it over me and my clothes —
And you had to pay for your own clothes for shows in those
     days —
And he slung the bucket at my head, and he said:
'IT'S YOUR LIFE IF YOU TRY THAT TOMORROW!' —
Thank you for the note Ted.

Tuesday night, I didn't look for clues . . .
but for some reason . . .
this was funnier – not doing anything —
They were out of control —
And I go up to Ted and say, 'Excuse me sir, but is this
    your cigarette lighter?'
And Ted —
the pupils of his eyes juddering like a washing-machine on
    final spin —
waits till he can be heard, then says:
'YES, IT IS – **YOU FUNNY LITTLE MAN!**' —
A bit of variation on the script, that was —
And so I arrested him . . . at a distance —
Luckily Margaret Thing had to bow between me and Ted —
and at the last bow, I sailed off the stage —
and beat the audience out of the auditorium doors —
and into the little pub up the road and round the corner,
    that the company never used —
But there to be found eventually by the director Bernard Kelly —
Bernard said, 'For Christ's sake, don't come in tomorrow —
Just come in a few minutes before your entrance and then
    GET OUT FAST before the bowing, or Ted Webster will
    kill you —
And oh shit!' said Bernard, 'The Bishop's coming again
    tomorrow' —
The Bishop coming a second time to a thriller? —
The Bishop used to come to the first night of everything —
and if it was a comedy, if it was a farce, yes – he'd be
    there every night —
except for Friday when he ran the jazz club —
(What he'd do you see, on the first night he could sort out where
    all the laughs were, so that on the next nights, when he'd always

bring a couple of cubs with him, you'd see them in the front row
and the Bishop'd go: 'UH HAHH! HA-HAHHH!! UH HA!!!
HA! HAHHH!!!! boys' – and on the last 'HAHHH!!!!' he'd
grab and squeeze their knees, cubs jumping and yelping —
He was training the younger members of the scout movement
in comedy timing.) —
I said, 'Bernard, is there some way of shutting an audience
up?' —
Bernard said, 'There's only one sure-fire technique for that —
What you'd have to do,' he said, 'is as soon as you come
on, forget your lines —
Just stand there and wait until the prompter's voice has rung
round the hall and then get on with it —
You won't get a murmur out of them then.'

So the next night, in the interests of survival, that's what I
did —
I simply came on and dried —
And they were as good as gold —
To be sure, it was a bit sad seeing the pale white knees
of the cubs in the front row —
ungrasped by Holy hand —
But that's what I did for the rest of the week's run —
I just came on and dried and we heard from the prompter
and everything was fine —
And Margaret Whatever-her-name-was came up to me after
the last show
and she said, 'I just want to congratulate you on your performance
Kenneth —
We were all so worried about it at the beginning of the week —
and then from somewhere —
you found such strength' —
'Thank you,' I said, humbly, thinking: arsehole.

A footnote on the Bishop of Colchester:
It seems that in his concluding couple of years on Earth he
   wasn't changing his underpants —
He'd originally put a pair on, but then he'd left them on
   until they'd disintegrated before donning the next pair —
We deduce this because, when he died, round the body was
   found eight elasticated bands —
And I had this picture, of the Bishop Up There —
with his left hand pulling his elastics up from his tubby body
   and plucking them with his right —

(He was a musical man, ran the jazz club.)

Captain Charlie Charrington
It was thus I first encountered the Captain:
When I was at the Royal Academy of Dramatic Art . . . there
    was a lady student there —
and I had designs on her doughnut —
She was the daughter of a handsome Indian doctor lady
    and some British chap —
and she had this heavy black hair which she chose to do
    up on the top of her head into a doughnut —
And when the classes got tedious, I'd find my attention wandering
    over to Dee Charrington and her doughnut of hair —
And you couldn't stop them: Playful imaginings . . .
Whackiest of which possibly was the Viciously Sharpened Shears
    Scenario —
the notion of stalking Dee Charrington through the dark-lit
    corridors of RADA with my shears —
coming up behind her and Zjip! Bong! Weee! —
I never mentioned this to her, of course —
nor to anyone come to that —
But I suppose she must have seen me looking at her in a
    rather interested fashion —
and this sparked up a bit of a friendship —
And so it was me she asked if I'd like to go with her to
    meet her father —
And this was odder than it sounds, because she'd never met
    her father —
Possibly she'd been viewed by him a couple of times as a
    toddler —
She wasn't sure —
Anyway, the fellow was to be appearing in the pub round
    the corner, the Marlborough, that lunchtime.

I had always regarded the bowler hat as the pinnacle of berkery —
But not as it sat on the head of Captain Charlie Charrington! —
To be sure, I think his bowler hat was curly of brim —
snapped down at the back —
But this was 1959 —
it was to be a good few years before Steed of *The Avengers*
    had one of those jobs —
And the Captain, he exuded a dash, a panache —
His daughter Dee was a wee bit nervous —
now powdering her nose for the second time —
And I was 19 and I said to the Captain, 'What do you do
    now then sir?' —
And Captain Charlie Charrington, of the twinkling eye, took
    my hand and put it inside his jacket —
And I felt his gun —
And I think it was the Captain's gun which fired my passion —
I began to woo the Captain's daughter in earnest now —
What I mean is, in her entirety —
It wasn't just her doughnut ring we were after now.

Sad to relate, she chose to marry another and go off to Canada
    with him, taking her mother and her brother with her.
Eight years later I was writing comedy sketches for the radio —
Monday Night at Home was the programme —
And I saw that the Ideal Home Exhibition was on and I said:
'Give us a ticket and I'll try and write something funny about
    that' —
Once into Olympia, I was halted by this particular stall —
Not that there was anything particular about the stall —

it was the salesman, the pitcher —
He was *mesmeric* —
All he was selling was saws —
But not saws of the usual variety —
These saws were sort of like string —
The notion being that you'd throw one end of your saw over
    an over-hanging bough, say, and Zzzzzzzzzzzzzzmmm! —
You'd saw it off —
But that wasn't the only use for these things, no —
Apparently the Gurkhas could take off a man's head in one
    with them —
they practised on goats —
And he was unloading these things like there was no tomorrow —
And you couldn't think that everyone had an over-hanging
    bough problem —
or were goat breeders with antisocial fantasies —
And there was an Indian gentleman there —
and he didn't know whether he wanted one or not —
And my new hero addresses him in an extremely foreign tongue:
'Yalla walah yillah walla yallah!' —
The fellow looked blank, so he tried him with another one:
'Rawah bawah hawah bah!' —
The fellow's still blank, but on the third one he gets him:
'Raggad ahab dallah halaba daha!' —
And the fellow went: 'Oyulla whahalla badah lilla badah ha?' —
'Oyuggah darrapah dag gadda oyehhh!' replies my man with
    mime of such drama it draws a gasp from the crowd and
    makes it difficult to walk —
and Indian fellow goes off with eight —
And then he saw me, the seller of saws saw me —
And he turned to his assistant and he said:
'We're closing for ten minutes' —
'You,' he said, 'are coming with me.'

And I followed him, I followed him out through a door which
    said NO EXIT —
and then up a darkened corridor to two mighty doors which
    said: NO ADMITTANCE —
and in we went —
And then we were in the exhibitors' canteen —
and he was getting a pot of tea for two, and a couple of
    chocolate éclairs —
and as we sat down he said:
'How's Dee?' —
The Captain! —
It was Captain Charlie Charrington, selling saws! —
'Oh! Well sir,' I said. 'I don't know —
She got married about seven or eight years ago —
went to Canada with this bloke' —
Yes yes yes! —
He had vaguely heard about this —
The Captain, he'd not seen her since that lunchtime in the pub —
Anyway, I was able to fill out the Captain's ten minutes with
    some images of his splendid daughter —
But given the fact that we'd mentioned her marriage, I was
    surprised by his last remark:
'Look after my Dee won't you,' he said —
'Yes sir,' I said, 'I will.'

And all of a sudden it was 1972 —
And it was that morning when I was supposed to be going
    to Munich —
(Why, you ask, would he be wanting to go to Munich?) —
Well, in those days I had my own travelling comedy outfit —
Ken Campbell's Roadshow —
And we were into international comedy now —
panging 40' of elastic into Sylveste McCoy's face, snipping off

the customers' ties: the comedy of driving nails up your nose,
   and putting live ferrets down your trousers —
International comedy —
And we were about to open a three-week residency in Munich's
   legendary Fuck-The-Hell Bar —
Actually I was just the director on that one —
but I had to be there because the ferret was on a one-way ticket —
due to the rabies laws —
I hoped I'd find some friendly Kraut who'd look after the
   little fellow when the show was over —
And also, I was getting the company to try a new routine
   in Munich —
I say it was a new routine —
as a matter of fact I'd pinched it from Abbot and Costello —
It's their baseball routine: *Who's On First Base*, they call it —
But I'd done a little work on it and put it into football terms —
It's a way of muddling the opposition by giving your team
   code names —
So our version went:
   'Who's on the left-wing,
   What's on the right-wing,
   I Don't Know is centre-forward' —
   Thick Person: 'Who's on the left-wing?' —
   Answer: 'Yes!'
Seven pages of this drivel, but you can get them hysterical
   with it —
Even Germans you can get hysterical with it.

(There were a couple of Israelis came to the Fuck-The-Hell
   Bar —
So impressed were they with this that they had the thing translated
   into Hebrew —

And they had me flown over to Tel Aviv to direct the
operations —
And I'll give you my Hebrew now:
'Mi bagaff hasmali,
Ma bagaff himani,
Ani lo yudiah haloutz ma kazi.
That's:
'Who's on the left-wing,
What's on the right-wing,
I Don't Know is centre-forward.'
And I've got another bit of Hebrew —
Before *'Mi bagaff hasmali, Ma bagaff himani, Ani lo yudiah*
haloutz ma kazi' got drummed into the director's head, I
worked up another one —
because in those days in Tel Aviv there seemed to be a lot
of Hebrew speakers who didn't know where they were —
They'd come up to me with their maps and their charts and
ask directions in a very demanding way —
I don't know why they thought I'd know the way —
but I thought it would be sporting if I could get rid of them
in Hebrew —
And I was in a café on the Dizengoff and the proprietor had
thoughtfully put in the menu helpful Hebrew phrases for the
visitor in phonetic English —
And I put together a slightly surreal reply for these occasions:
'Ani rotzah lekuleff tapuzeem.'
Which translates as: 'Excuse me, I wish to peel oranges.'
So when I got asked directions now, I'd say:
'Ani rotzah lekuleff tapuzeem!' —
Sometimes I think they'd hear my English accent coming through
and reply: 'Really? What – right away old boy?'
'Ani rotzah lekuleff tapuzeem!' —
'But you're not a woman!'
'What? No no. That's true, I'm not a woman, no . . . but this
is a country, young as it is, where a man may peel an orange,
isn't it?' —

'No no no,' he said. ' "*Ani rotzah*" is the feminine form; what you're saying there is "I, *a lady*, wish to peel oranges." ')

Anyway, I'd missed the first train-boat-train to Munich due to some farce in Dave Hill's kitchen the night before —

And I seemed to be doing nothing about catching the second one —

And it wasn't like it was going to be dull company in Munich —

Marcel Steiner had just invented his smallest theatre in the world —

his two-seater theatre he'd built on the side-car of his motor-bike —

And Alan Devlin was going to be there doing his comedy drunk heckling if he wasn't too pissed —

And then I realized I was paralysed —

I assumed it was terminal —

And the phrase that came to mind was: Entropy of the bone marrow —

That's what I'd got —

And that's why I missed the midnight train —

I can remember looking at myself in the mirror, and saying:

'You're all hollowed out Kenif —

It's all gone a-crumble' —

And the only thing working was the elbows —

And so I levered myself up by the elbows —

and I elbowed myself to bed, falling eventually into a stiff sleep —

to be awoken about 3 o'clock in the morning by the telephone ringing —

And it was Dee Charrington phoning me from Toronto —

And she wanted to be talking about her father —

'Your father Dee?' I said. 'You mean the Captain.' —

And just saying those words: 'The Captain!' —

It flushed all the entropy out of the bone marrow —

and I was ready for anything —
Dee informed me that her father the Captain had died —
He'd died in mysterious circumstances in Oman —
and the body had now been flown back to England —
And neither she nor her mother could attend the funeral (which
   was to be on the Thursday) and could I stand in for them? —
I said, 'Well yes. Yes, I'd be pleased to do that for you, Dee.' —
In that event, would I ring this telephone number —
the number of a certain Doris Kontardi —
Doris Kontardi had accompanied the Captain's body back to
   England —
I said, 'Well, it's about half-past three in the morning now Dee —
Shall I leave it till later?' —
She'd got a Canadian voice now —
She said, *'I'd rather you rang now.'*

So there we are, the Captain dead —
Died in mysterious circumstances in Oman —
And now, phoning up Doris Kontardi —
And speaking to a veddy posh voice —
Veddy posh people put dees where their arrs should be —
So not 'very' but 'veddy' —
And not 'Doris' but 'Doddis': Doddis Kontardi —
And she, Doddis Kontardi, was an archaeologist lady, and
   she'd been commissioned by the Sultan of Oman to dig up
   stuff round Muskat to stock a little museum there for the
   tourists —
And her archaeological site facilitator —
known (wonderfully) locally as Sheik Fixit —
had been Captain Charlie Charrington —
Evidently ideal for the position since he knew every nuance
   of Arabic from Morocco to the Gulf —
'But,' said Doddis, 'there'd been film people there —

and there'd been something of a party —
and everybody had wanted the Captain to stay —
But he'd met an old friend, and he'd said —
'*No, there is something I must do.*' —
And he'd gone off into the desert with the old friend —
And we don't think it was the heart attack which was fatal —
It was the fall backwards on the rocks . . .' —
But there was doubt in Doddis Kontardi's voice as to whether
   that is what had really happened —
She said, 'Will Dee be coming to the funeral, and her mother?' —
I said, 'No no, I'm afraid they can't make it, —
they've asked me to stand in for them.'
But then, with inspiration, I said:
'But maybe her brother will come – maybe Paul will come' —
She said: '*The Captain had a son*??!' —
'Well,' I said, 'I'm not *totally* sure about that —
Maybe he didn't —
I don't know —
But if he did, his name might be Paul —
I think —
But as I say, I'm not sure' —

Then back to Dee —
I said, 'That Kontardi's very worried about the *existence* of
   your brother Paul' —
She said,'Paul will be there —
Can he stay with you?' —
Yeah, sure —
And Paul arrived and I said:
'How well did you know your father Paul?' —
He said, 'I met him on four occasions —
Once when I was five, once when I was eleven, once when
   I was fifteen, and once when I was nineteen' —

I said: 'When did you first feel the gun?' —
He said: 'I first felt the gun when I was five —
I felt the gun again when I was eleven —
And when I was eleven I was also shown the uncut gems, and
    pointed to the X marking the spot on a certain Island in the
    South Pacific —
Also I was instructed this way:
that if our paths were ever to chance to meet, I must never
    call the man "Dad" or "Father" —
the name was always to be Charlie, or —
The Captain.'

Crossword enthusiasts will know this, that the favourite anagram
    in the *Guardian* for 'funeral' is 'real fun' —
And so it was with the Captain's —
A proper burial for the Captain —
and four weeping women round the grave:
Doddis; a chummy lady name of Sammy; and a Venus in
    Furs (Gwendoline) —
And the Captain had been living with the three of them at
    the same time —
but unbeknown to each other —
And they all met round the grave —
And the Venus in Furs had brought along several male shoulders
    to swoon and to weep on —
but not Sammy, and not Doddis —
And so Paul and I took them off to the pub for a nostalge
    about the Captain —
leaving behind the fourth lady —
We never got to know who she was —
the lone and anonymous griever at the graveside —
In the Pub, Doddis silent with her gin —
one supposes hurt by the rude discovery of the Captain's two,

possibly three, other ladies —
But Sammy recalling for us the first time she met the Captain —
In Aden . . . a military airfield —
and to her it was just so *wonderful* that such a *wonderful*
   man had found any time at all for her —
And Doddis softens —
(and Sammy will move in with Doddis, together the better
   to keep bright the Captain's memory.)

The reading of the will had its moment —
the Captain had left his effects variously between Doddis, and
   Sammy, and the Venus in Furs —
but with this proviso: that were it to chance that the three of
   them all snuffed it within six months of the reading of the
   will —
in that event, another envelope must be opened —
'Paul!' I said, 'What a Dad! What a funeral! —
I wouldn't have missed that for anything! —
We must keep in touch!' —
And I waved him off on the plane back to Toronto.

Six months later I was watching the first run of *The Exor-
   cist* —
Remember it? —
The Exorcist begins with an archaeological dig —
'Northern Iraq' it says, and there's a bunch of Arabs digging —
   and then there's the call to prayer —
And then we're snaking through the archaeological site with
   the little Arab boy —
Boy suddenly stops and through his spread little Arab legs

we see Max von Sydow —
And Max is portraying the archaeological site facilitator —
(the Sheik Fixit if you like) —
And the little boy's saying in Arabic (there are subtitles):
'They've found something!' —
Now with the Arab archaeologist, and he is saying to Max:
    'Some interesting finds. Lamps, arrowheads, coins.' —
MAX (*examining some crap*): 'Strange . . . not of the same
    period' —
Max, scrabbling up crevice pulls out appalling object —
too appalling for us to be allowed to look at properly yet —
Cut to the café —
It's two hours later
(Two hours later! —
Max von Sydow has aged twenty years!) —
Max is on heart tablets now —
And then we're in that little museum —
in heavy Arab company, talking Arabic —
'Shatan', we hear the word: 'Shatan' —
'Evil against evil,' we read —
Max is fiddling with another (or the same) appalling object
    which stops the clock! —
Heavy Arab says, 'I wish you didn't have to go' —
MAX: 'There is something I must do.'

Now driving towards archaeological site —
Halted by Arabs in flowing white robes with guns —
(Arabs relax a bit when they see it's Max)
Max allowed onto site —
And that's when you see it! —
Maybe you glimpsed it before —
but not like this! —

the dog-dragon statue! —
And there's wild dogs fighting themselves to death down there —
and then there's the Sun going down behind the statue —
(Ugh!) —
The statue! —
Max! —
Statue! —
Max! —

Cut to Georgetown, USA.

That line: 'There is something I must do' is redundant in
   the movie —
in fact it's confusing —
What did Max von Sydow have to do? —
Go and watch the sun go down on a statue? —
Or does it refer to his book, maybe? —
Do you remember the plot of the thing? —
Once we've left the desert, we're in Georgetown, USA, and
   it's all about this little American girl and how her head keeps
   twiddling right round, and she can't stop spitting green stuff
   at vicars —
Then someone says, 'Hey – we haven't seen Max von Sydow
   for nearly an hour now —
Let's go and see what he's doing —
Maybe he could help!' —
And we find Max, now living in Woodstock, USA and in
   the middle of writing a book —
And so that's what he must have meant by 'There is something
   I must do':

'I must just watch the sun set on that statue, and then get out
of here, maybe rent a cottage in somewhere like Woodstock
and write a book'.

I was on the phone to Paul in Toronto —
'Have you seen *The Exorcist*?' —
He said, 'Yeah man I have. And listen: that was the Captain's
dig!' —
"Northern Iraq?" Bollocks! —
The whole thing was shot in Muskat, Oman' —
That the Captain was working for *The Exorcist* film company
as well as for Doddis —
He was batting round Oman in a helicopter finding locations
for them —
That Max von Sydow bases his characterization on Captain
Charlie Charrington —
Those are actually the Captain's heart tablets in the café scene! —
And that museum you see there, that's Kontardi's museum! —
And it was a party for *The Exorcist* film crew and company,
when they'd all wanted him to stay, but the captain had said:
'*No, there is something I must do*' —
and had gone off into the desert with his old friend —
and to his death —
And that his death had been unspeakably weirder than a heart
attack —
that Doris Kontardi had had to spread a lot of money around
Muskat to buy that certificate —
and be permitted to fly her Captain back to England —
And that line, 'There is something I must do,' is in that film as
a mark of respect and love for Captain Charlie Charrington.

I would suggest that there is a hole in the plotting of *The Exorcist*:
How did the appalling object get from Northern Iraq to the
 bottom of some stairs in Georgetown, USA?

Were you with me in my kitchen now, I would be introducing
 you to this 'old friend' —

This Dog-dragon figurine (9″) —
You'd note the Dog-dragon snouting —
(and that this snouting would be even more impressive if it
   hadn't been part snapped-off somewhere in its history) —
And the cloak-cum-wing effect there at the back —
I would suggest to you that had we the magic of movie effects
   we could put the breeze up folk with this thing as effectively
   as the one in *The Exorcist* —
And I can tell you how this got to the bottom of my garden —
(Haverstock Hill, 1981) —
It was like this:
I was directing the Czech comedy *War with the Newts* at the
   Riverside Studios Hammersmith and we'd broken rehearsals
   for the day and I was passing Olympia —
And on at Olympia now was the 'Mind and Body' Exhibition —
the 'New Age' effort —
and there'd been some humour there in previous years, so
   I decided to potter in —
But actually it was rather tacky that year —
There was a MacDonald's —
and I found the whole thing doubtful —
e.g. crystal pendulums —
just expensive things on strings really —
but you'd be able to find lost stuff with them was the claim —
they start twiddling the other way round when you near your
   lost thing —
And buried treasure too! —
All you need do is DANGLE IT OVER A MAP and it'll
   jerk about when it's over anything interesting —
What bollocks! —
And this dame offering to look sideways into the iris of your
   eyes, and prescribe exactly what stuff you ought to be sniffing
   in order to release your potential —
Three Rotherham Buddhists insisting if you chant 'Nam Yoho
   Bother Um' several hours a morning and eat and drink

nothing but carrot for a month you wouldn't have any more
problems —
Bollocks —
and dangerous bollocks! —
But I was halted by the last stall to the left of the exit —
which was a stall of magic wands . . .
Not the kind of wand a stage conjuror would use —
These were 'Earth Magic Wands for Successful Magic':

> *'Wands must always be culled at dawn or dusk, when the*
> *Sun's rays strike the trees from the side and not from above.*
> *And it gives a marvellous feeling to be in a deep wood at first*
> *light with all the trees excitedly jostling about you, offering their*
> *branches for magical use. In minutes my arms are full and I*
> *have to decline the rest as gracefully as possible so as not to*
> *cause offence.'*

These wands (and very weird they were) are individually hand-
crafted by the stall proprietor Dusty Miller —
'These wands,' I found myself asking Mr Miller, 'would they
be useful in the directing of Czechoslovakian comedy?' —
'Is that what you do?' he said —
'Well, it's what I'm doing at the moment,' I said —
He said, 'More than likely' —
I said, 'Well could you steer me to a wand that might be
useful for that purpose then?' —
'No,' he said, 'I can't do that. I can't do that because you
have to let the wand choose you.' —
So I stood in front of all these wands —
Seeing if one wanted me —
And there was this really *wicked* wand, and I was thinking,
'Go on! You have me!' —
But it went all queeny on me —
'No,' it was saying. 'No-oo' (campily) —
But the one that seemed to have its eye (!) on me . . .
I guess we've all popped along to the zoo in springtime in

order to see a baboon's erection? —
The first erection of spring? —
When it's pencil thin with the wonger on the top? —
And when they first notice them, these baboons, they don't
    know what they're for —
They ping them at each other —
They think perhaps they've been summoned to some sort of
    novelty conker tournament —
It's not until they've got the mauve bots that they know what
    they're for . . .
But this is not going to turn into a David Attenborough
    evening —
What I wanted to say was that the wand that wanted me
    was like a male baboon's donger in early May —
'P'raps that one,' I said, pointing —
'Hmmm,' said Dusty, 'could be a match —
But look, about these wands —
Do try and keep it with you at all times, at least for the first
    month – until we find out whether it gets on with you or not.' —
And if it didn't get on with me, he'd give me my five pounds
    back, or exchange it for another wand —
I left with it inside my jacket —
Out, it would have excited comment —
possibly arrest.

Lurking outside the Olympia portals was an old chum, Richard
    Kilgour, composer —
But the reason he was there was because a couple of weeks
    before, he'd parted with £250 to the Silva Mind Control
    outfit who had a stall in the Exhibition —
The Silva Mind Control, Kilgour tells me, train you up in a
    system called 'Dream Mirroring' —
and if you apply yourself fully to that for some weeks, you

find that you've so tuned your mind up that you only have
to visualize something and you get it —
'Well for £250 Richard,' I said, 'that's a snip if it really works —
Oh look,' I said. (A poster.) 'Bob Dylan's on at Earl's Court
tonight —
Shall we go and see Bob Dylan?' —
'No,' he said. 'We wouldn't get in. It'll be all booked up' —
I said, 'Actually we might – I've got a magic wand,' (giving
him a peek at the beast) —
'Oh,' he said. 'Well it'd be a handy opportunity for me to
try out my visualizing' —
And so off to Earl's Court, and a battle of the sorcerers:
Richard takes up position on the corner of side road opposite
Earls Court, eyes upwards behind lids, awful bit of eye-white
beneath pupil showing —
and humming pottily, attempts visualization of Bob Dylan
tickets —
I go on to next road, wait till moment is right —
Out with naughty wand! Waving!!
'Two tickets Bob Dylan!'
and this fellow comes running up —
sold me two tickets —
I said, 'I'll give you another fiver if you take these two tickets
and give them to that man with his eyes shut over there! —
If he says anything, don't say anything back! —
just come on like you're a deaf mute or something! Hubba
bubba hubba bubba!'
Chap agrees.

Richard comes over to me with the tickets. He is *shaken* —
'Wow man!' he said. 'I'd just got them visualized and this
spastic came up to me and thrusts them at me!' —
Even weirder, being only a junior in the Silva Mind Control, he

hadn't liked to bother the aetheric with anything excessive, so
he'd only dared to visualize back row seats —
And that's exactly what he got!

Once in Earl's Court, I had the wand out and proud —
And this fellow came running up to me and he said: 'Can
    I see your ticket?' —
I said: 'Certainly' —
'Oo,' he said. 'That's a crappy ticket! —
You can sit with me, my friend hasn't come' —
And so we went with this guy (me and the wand) —
second row seats us, Bob Dylan —
Richard had to go to the back —
It was all he'd visualized —
I thought, Wow, this wand likes me! It gets on with me! —
I slept with it, of course, and the next morning was Sunday —
and I thought: I'll clear my shed out today, and I put the
    wand on the window ledge of the shed to supervise —
and I was humping stuff out of the shed and I kept passing,
    embedded in the lawn, what I took to be my little daughter
    Daisy's upturned chalk boat —
I thought, What chalk boat? She hasn't got a chalk boat! —
And then I thought: – I don't think I've ever seen a chalk boat —
I pringed it out of the lawn, and it was this Dog-dragon figurine —
The moment I picked it up, I saw clearly in my mind's eye —
(I rationalize that it's *The Exorcist* connection) —
the dashing phiz of Captain Charlie Charrington —
I chummed the figurine with the wand on the window ledge —
At first I took it to be a novelty chess piece – that was
    my theory —
I assumed the neighbours had been playing novelty chess —
and got so pissed off with it they'd hurled the novelty chess
    pieces about the gardens —

But as the day wore on I knew it was no novelty chess piece,
  this —
I thought: I'd really like to show this to Dusty Miller —
And it was the last day of the Mind and Body Exhibition —
I sped back to Olympia —
'Mr Miller,' I said, 'two tickets for Bob Dylan, that's one thing —
But what do you make of this?' —
and showed him the Dog-dragon —
He took it —
He held it professionally —
He said, 'Well I don't think it means *you* any harm —
But if I were you I'd have it checked out by the Black Magic
  artefact couple over there —' —
Who turned out to be an hysterical pair —
They were Whoopsie people —
And they bred enormous snakes and had a coven in Willesden
  every Thursday —
And they offered to whoopsie off with the Dog-dragon and
  get the next Thursday's coven to psychometrize it and find
  out more about it —
And I thought, Well how exciting, yeah okay —
But the coven uncovered nothing —
And so they took it to the British Museum —
And the British Museum said, 'Well we don't know what it is —
We think it was made in perhaps the late 1700s —
but for what purpose we really couldn't tell you' —
Meanwhile, Dusty Miller said, 'When you get back see if there
  are any more —
Sometimes when you find one, you find more' —
I hadn't got a lot of faith in that actually —
And it was dusk when the wand and I got back,
and I thought I knew this little bit of garden, but —
whoopsie —
I saw it almost right away —
A little pyramid of white coming up through the lawn —
And I got a trowel and dug it up with extreme care —

And it was this: Exhibit Two: the Pair of Legs (5″) —

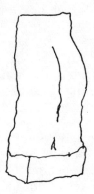

Draped legs —
Or maybe they're legs behind a curtain —
And then the next day, I found the Shrieking Monk top half
      (4″) —

for many the freakiest of the set —
This loop of wire in the mouth . . . —
What is that? —

Presumably he's shrieking: 'Coul' sonhwonh ge' 'is fu' wire
ou' o' 'y 'ou', 'lease!' —
Sometimes people think that the Shrieking Monk belongs to
the Legs —
Honestly, we think it's doubtful —
He doesn't fit them —
But also, if you had his loop-of-wire-in-the-mouth problem,
it's unlikely that you'd be standing quite like *that* —
and the Legs on their own are sinister —
the Monk top half, ghastly —
But stick them together and it's a silly whoopsie man —
'What a beautiful day, brothers, for putting a loop of wire
in your mouth, doing a whoopsie behind the curtain, and
shouting "Wire (why're) we slaves of our habits?!" '

'FOKWAEA' is a Pidgin word —
(Pidgin English – the language of the South Pacific) —
I first came on the word in the phrase 'Bigman Jif blong
   Fokwaea Aelan' —
'Aelan' means 'island'; 'Bigman Jif' is the 'chief' – or 'squire'
   we might say —
'blong' here is 'of' —
So: 'The Squire of Fokwaea Island' —
'Fokwaea' (note the influence of Irish on Pidgin here) is 'barbed
   wire'!

In the cast of *Warp*, the World's Longest Play, (see Guinness
   Book of Records years 1981, 1982, 1983) which I directed,
   we had the services of young actor David DeNil —*
And David DeNil was the most minimal person I have ever
   encountered —
I will recall for you how he used to smoke a cigarette:
There would be barely sufficient energy in those fingers to
   hold the cigarette —
any less, and the fag would have dropped on the carpet —
And the lips too: minimal energy there —
And his walk was such that it caused minimum alarm to insect
   life —
I couldn't have him do too much in the show, because apart
   from all that, he was totally inaudible —
'I suppose there's no chance of you speaking up David?!!' —

*The video of the original *Warp* production – all 18 hours of it, plus some other novelties Neil has
bunged on for the seeker – may be purchased for £100 (plus P & P) from the author: Neil Oram,
Goshem, Grotaig, Bunloit Road, Near Drumnadrochil, Invernessshire, Scotland.

What can't you hear me? —
'No, we can't hear **anything!**' —
But I found a remarkable use for the guy, because it turned
    out that he had the legendary Minus Quality —
i.e., if he left the room, the stage looked somehow fuller —
And it was a terrific way of starting off a scene —
You'd have David leave —
and it was like turning up the pink light.

Anyway, what I want to tell you: the show was up and running,
    and a sensation —
And I'd gone to bed and I was asleep and I'd started to dream —
And then this chap *barged into my dream*, and he said:
'You know that David DeNil feller who's in your production?' —
I said, 'Yes?' . . . He said, 'What he's got to do is this:
He's got to go and see every live show that Ken Dodd gives
    for a year —
Will you tell him?' —
I said, 'Yes, alright,' and then he left and I was allowed to
    get on with my dream —
And I went flying I think, and whatnot —
But then this dream wound up in the South Pacific —
and my late mother was roped to a window sill —
and I was just cutting her free, when this chap turned up again —
He said, 'You won't forget to tell David, will you?' —
I said, 'I'm just rescuing my mother!' —
But this chap and his demands were in my mind when I woke
    up in a way that I think no dream should ever be —
(I don't think it's healthy) —
When I went into the theatre that evening, there was David —
He was minimally applying his make-up —
He wasn't due on for an hour yet —
for his first exit —

'Ah David,' I said. 'I had a dream about you last night —
In fact I was instructed as to what you've got to do with
    your future —
I don't know what you think about these things, but it seems
    to me that if you ask me what it was, then you've got to do
    it —
But if you don't, you won't' —
And David said, 'Thank you' —
And he didn't ask me! —
Until we got to the pub, and he said, 'What is it I've got to do?' —
'What you've got to do David, is see every live show that
    Ken Dodd gives for a year.' —
'Thank you,' said David —
And then later he said: Would it be alright if I don't start till January?' —
I said I thought January would be fine —
And January saw him taking off to Southport —
He hadn't got much money, so he borrowed an arctic sleeping-
    bag —
and he slept on Southport beach under the pier —
Doddy was doing his pantomime there —
David was on the beach for more than a week —
until he made some minimal friends who let him sleep on
    their floor —
He showed the box office manageress what little money he'd
    got, and she gave him a serial ticket so he could see all the
    shows —
That's twice daily —
three times on a Wednesday —
three times on a Saturday —
And he didn't miss any of them! —
And then he got two weeks off —
And then Ken Dodd was doing a tour of cities and towns
    of the North of England —
David kept with that tour; didn't miss one performance, and
    at the end of the tour, Ken Dodd has a little party on the
    stage —

And David DeNil has the courage not only to attend the
party, but go up and introduce himself to Ken Dodd, and
tell the man what he's doing —
i.e., his intention is to see every live show Doddy gives for
a year —
And that this was down to a dream which a friend of his
had had —
Ken Dodd said: 'Well David, I think you may have problems
with my next engagement.'
David asked why —
And Dodd said, 'Because it's in the New Hebrides: F-Farty!' —
And when Dodd said 'F-Farty!' David took this to be some
Scouse expression meaning 'Be off with you!' —
But David couldn't see what the problem was going to be —
He'd got the date of this gig, and presumably he'd have to
apply himself in good time to the relevant Scottish ferry —
But then he couldn't find the *New* Hebrides on the map —
Up there by Scotland, there's Outer Hebrides and Inner Heb-
rides, but no *New* Hebrides —
For the New Hebrides you turn left at Fiji —
And the capital of the New Hebrides is Efaté Island —
And David ran —
My expression meaning David would now do anything for
money —
Anything!! —
And he knocked it up, he knocked up the required sum —
And we waved him goodbye —
Off to Efaté Island —
Flying by way of Sydney, Australia —
And we got a postcard back from David —
and it seemed it was quite a lark on Efaté Island —
He'd met some very nice Australians —
he'd also been interviewing gentlemen with feathers in their
noses —
But listen, he'd been to the yacht club, he'd been to the
three hotels, he'd been to all the bars —

And nobody had heard of Ken Dodd!

But David was to become famous on Efaté Island as the Man
  Looking For Ken Dodd —
He knew all the gags, he knew all the routines —
People would say, 'Well who is this Ken Dodd then?' —
And David could go on till next morning —
The language spoken on Efaté Island, and on all the islands
  of the New Hebrides, and in the Solomon Islands, and Papua
  New Guinea, and more —
the inter-island language, the *lingua franca*, is Pidgin English —
This is no more than 1,500 words of English (quaintly mutated
  and oddly spelled) —
but with cunning, you can steer them to almost any concept —
And it only takes about a week to pick up Pidgin, and David
  was now amusing himself by translating Ken Dodd's routines
  into Pidgin for the entertainment of the natives —
And there was a bunch of natives and they were going to be
  canoeing off the next morning to visit their more primitive
  cousins on Ambrym and Malekula, and on to the Solomon
  Islands —
They wondered if David would like to come with them —
'Oo yes please' —
On Malekula the chaps had their bollocks swinging free but
  their pricks in wrappers —
they were soon informed that tonight was to be a special
  evening —
the sort of evening you'd really got to tog up for —
So they hummed away the afternoon, painting their legs up,
  putting on their clankers and sticking their danglers in —
And then when they were sat about under the banyan tree
  they were all introduced to David DeNil —
And David DeNil launched into the first gag of his Pidgin

Dodd routine —
And the Bigman Chief of the Island called for him to halt —
and go back and tell it again —
And then halt, and go back and tell it again —
And he told it five times —
But on the fifth time of telling the whole Island held its sides
    and howled away the night in laughter! —
And the next day he was canoed on to the next island —
Listen, he toured nineteen islands with one gag! —
And this is it:

> *'Im fulugud dei. Im fulugud dei blong yumitufala*
> *pushem lilfala salwata wanae*
> *insaed postofis letahol blong praeafala pasta*
> *talim – "ski aelan twinki twink plantifala ia!" '*

You'll notice that David took a liberty with Dodd's text here:
'Lilfala salwata wanae' —
that's because there aren't actually cucumbers as such on the
    islands —
I'm sure you could probably steer your way, circumnavigate
    Pidgin and arrive at the concept of cucumberishness —
But it could take all afternoon —
For example the word for piano is:
'Bigfala bokis blong Waetman; tut blong im – sam i blak,
    sam i waet – yu kilim emi singaot' —
Bokis = box; *tut* = teeth —
Kilim isn't 'kill,' it's only 'hit'. —
If you want to say 'kill', you have to say: *'Kilim altageta*
    ded finis yeah!' —

Doddy's song *Love is Like a Violin* would come out as,
'Lavem laekem lilfala bokis – sipos yu skrasem beli – emi
    kraeout' —

So for cucumber David took the easy way out, and went for
   the *'lilfala salwata wanae'* concept —
'Little fellow salt water one-eye' —
And actually not such a little fellow —
you might encounter one whilst paddling off a Solomon Island —
It's a species of Solomon Island sea slug —
If you do see one, whip it out the water – they're long brown
   things with a luminous green streak —
Whip it out, and give it a clout and it'll cough up a bit of
   khaki unpleasantness and then go limp —
and you can toss it onto the beach and it'll dry out, and you
   can grind it up and make a fishy pepper to sprinkle on your
   yams.

David's gag would come in one of Doddy's 'What a beautiful
   day' routines.
'What a beautiful day for running into Woolworths and shouting:
   "Tescos"!' —
'What a beautiful day for putting your kilt on upside down,
   standing on your head and shouting: "How's that for a shuttle-
   cock!" ' —
So —
Im fulugud dei – What a beautiful day —
blong – for ('blong' is all the prepositions)
yumitufala – we, us (lit. 'You-me-two-fellows')
pushem lilfala salwata wanae – to shove a little salt water
   one-eyed chappy
insaed postofis letahol – into the letterbox
blong praeafala pasta – belonging to the vicar

talim – *'ski aelan twinki twink plantifala ia!'* – tell him 'the
sky island twinkle twinkle people are here!'
Dodd's original: 'What a beautiful day for shoving a cucumber
in the vicar's letterbox and shouting: "The Martians have
arrived!" '

David's also locally revered as the fala who introduced Limerick
form to the islands —
This I think is one of his best efforts:

> *'Runemfala flaengfokis*
> *Bol defren habig, no mokis!*
> *Wan bol smol*
> *Nomo no bol,*
> *Narafala bigfala: winim praes bokis':*

runemfala – a hunter (with a spear) —
flaeng fokis – flying fox —
bol – 'ball', or 'balls'. (They don't bother with S's for plurals
out there – you have to know it by context. I happen to know
that in this case it's 'balls'.)
Habig – size, sizes (lit. 'how big') —
bol defren habig – balls of different sizes —
No mokis – no laughter! —
Wan bol smol – one ball small —
Nomo no bol – almost no ball —
Narafala – the other one —
bigfala – a big one —
Winim praes bokis – wins him prize boxes —
(It's always the same prize every year on the Solomon Islands,
but they pay a great deal of attention to the mud-and-wicker
box it comes in) —
David, probably recalling there the young sport from Devizes —

'. . . *Whose balls were of different sizes,*
One ball was small,
Almost no ball at all,
But the other was large and won prizes.'

But I think the more enchanting in David's Pidgin.

According to David, the rudest word on the islands is '*hambag*' —
which means unnatural unsanctioned sex with an underage girl
    to whose father you haven't given six pigs —
Apparently the British Council had funded Dame Edith Evans
    to do her one woman favourite snippets show round the
    islands —
The first clanger might have been that women performing at all
    is contrary to custom, but they'd thought she was a bloke —
But when she'd given her *Importance of Being Earnest* she'd
    had to canoe for it —

Anyway, we learn all this sort of thing when David at length
    returns from his Solomon Islands adventure —
His greeting is strange:
he doesn't shake your hand, or kiss you or anything usual —
he grabs you by the upper arm and gives it a squeeze —
And evidently that is a Solomon Islands greeting —
a throwback to the good old days —
(They were eating each other on a regular basis up until about
    1935) —
And apparently the upper arm is the second tastiest part of
    a person —

So the greeting means literally: 'Hmmm . . . so far so good
   . . . like to know you better!' —
And another thing: David is no longer minimal —
This dates from his falling in love on the islands —
It's not only feathers they put in their noses —
they put all sorts of stuff there: pencils, pens, cigarettes, cigars —
But David had, on the island of Ambrym encountered the
   apprentice priestess of some cargo cult —
and she'd so worked on her nasal cartilage that she could
   snap it over items like soup tins, harpic containers —
and play them —
(make a good novelty act with the Bishop, that) —
But David was in a bit of a dilemma: —
Was he **really** in love with her? —
or was he merely in love with the idea of introducing her
   to his mother? —
Either way, he realized it was all up now with his minimalism.

David handed me a properly made out bill —
invoicing me for £3,000; I said, 'Good Lord, what's this
   David?' —
He said, 'Well, look I didn't fulfil your commission as
   worded —
– i.e., I didn't go and see every live show that Ken Dodd
   gave for a year —
But bringing all this stuff back, doesn't it open some doors
   for you?' —
'Yes,' I said. 'Yes David, maybe it does —
But there's no sense in which I *commissioned* you to do
   anything —
I merely had the goodness to tell you what some geezer
   who barged into my dream *told* me to tell you' —
'Yeah,' he said, and he was going round my place picking

stuff up —
not like he was looking for clues —
it was more like he had all the evidence he required —
He had plans for returning to the islands, he said —
probably offering himself for the hundred day circumcision
   ritual —
and then thus cleansed, claiming the trainee priestess —
(She wasn't just somewhere to stick your old tins —
she was a loving, caring woman —
And his for six pigs! —)
'There's homosexuality on the islands,' he said —
'O,' I said. 'Well there's homosexuality here, I believe.' —
'Yes,' he said, 'but here it's optional.'
And as he was leaving he turned to me and said:
'So carry on up your own arsehole then' —
And he was gone —
And I thought, Wow – that's a really big man's just gone
   out of here —
And I really experienced envy —
I really envied him his journey —
how far he'd got —
what he might do next —
The Bigman Jif blong Fokwaea Aelan . . .

The Melvyn Bragg Show once took a passing interest in my
  Two-Faced Acting Classes —
And I still do them —

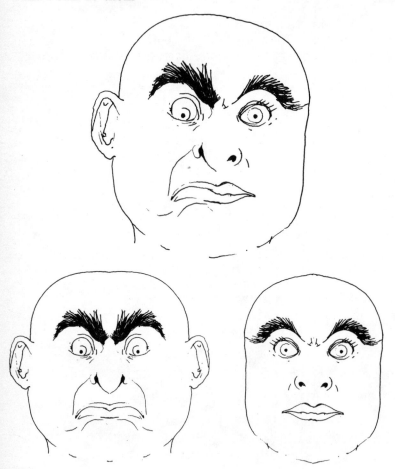

but now I call it my Enantiodromic Approach to Drama —
and charge a lot more money for it —
The Enantiodromic Approach is simply the study of how one
    side of the face is different from the other —
They're different people —
You can look at one side of a chap's face and say, 'It's the
    face of a serial killer' —
and then you look at the other and it's got something of
    Mother Theresa about it —
And the answer is of course that it's both —
A face is composed of two contradictory, mutually exclusive
    facets —
And my Enantiodromic classes help you stress your contra-
    dictions —
Under laboratory scrutiny, it seems that my right facet is that
    of a vacant inept housewife called Elsie —
And the left side is my Spanking Squire side —
The Spanking Squire —
he's into the chastisement of the young ladies of the village
    whether they've been naughty or not —
I find this is useful knowledge not only in performing but in life —
encountering real people —
When meeting women for the first time, I know to present
    them with my Elsie side —
I mumble and burble through her, and they're really much
    happier with that —
It's not till much later in the relationship that I play my Spanking
    Squire!

When I do this as a live show it's about now that I sense a
    rumble in the house of what I call 'stage property angst' —
I schlepp about with me quite a load of gear —
on the stage with me will be my photo of Stuart Pearce;

Dog-dragon, Monk and Legs; the complete paperback works
of Philip K. Dick; a map of London with pins in it; a ball of
wool; mouldering 10″ × 8″ of the Fuck-The-Hell Bar; Ken
Dodd's routines in Pidgin on big boards; tickling sticks; a
curly brim bowler; ladies' clothes and wig; and more —
As I move through my subjects I move through my objects —
the props serving to both authenticate and prompt —
It's my Doddis museum —
an extension of the Gearies Friday Showtime —
·and there are these three major items I haven't mentioned yet:
    Balinese Wooden Frog and Umbrella carving (4½′) —
    Fur Bugs Bunny Disguised in toad mask (5′) —
    And a Melanesian Ken Dodd Idol (4½′) —
The Melanesian Dodd is such a sensation that it is in disguise —
It's wearing a Papua New Guinea wartyfala mask —
and I don't reveal its true identity till the very end of the show —
anyway, if I've sensed the 'property angst' —
that people think they've tumbled how the show works now —
'He's got to go round and he's got to pick everything up
    and he's got to show us it all before we can go home' —
then I'll get a load of things handled and out of the way —
For example, the three big items, I'll explain, simply tell us
    that this is part of a trilogy —
The first part was *Furtive Nudist*, sometimes called *The Recollec-
    tions of a Furtive Nudist* – and the logo, the three dimensional
    totem of *Furtive Nudist* was the Frog —
'Here's tonight's gent,' I say, drawing attention to the Melanesian
    Doddy in warty masquerade —
'featured mascot of *Pigspurt – or Six Pigs from Happiness*' —
'And this' – (Bugs Bunny) – 'will be the totem of part three,
    Jamais Vu —
One predicts that at the climax of *Jamais Vu* when I remove
    the toad mask' —
– (doing so) —
'revealing Bugs Bunny, —
there won't be a dry seat in the house'.

Do you know the expression 'jamais vu'? —
Well 'déjà vu' – English expression, French words —
Déjà vu is when you arrive somewhere you've never been
    before and think: *I've been here before* . . .
Jamais vu is when you go home, and you say *Christ I've
    never been here before*! —
I will of course be dealing with jamais vu in its extreme form —
That's when you go home, say *Christ I've never been here
    before and I'm not even here now*! —
There was a stirring case of jamais vu last year in Scotland —
A Dundee girl had jamais vu on her father —
Father came in from work and she thought: *That's not my
    father*! —
She had jamais vu on him, you see —
And she came to the opinion that he was an android —
And to prove the point she pulled his throat out to expose
    the wires! —
And she was wrong —
It may not have been her father, I don't know, but it certainly
    wasn't a robot —
And of course Derek —
Derek and his mum who chopped him up —
Possibly a case of jamais vu there.

People think, Oh Christ he's going to have to read all those
    books to us! —
But no no no. This is just my collection of the works of
    the late American author Philip K. Dick —

That's because I'm what is known in science fiction circles
   as a 'Dickhead' —
We Dickheads are divided into two camps —
There are those who'll tell you: 'Only read the books he wrote
   before 1974, all the later stuff's crap!' —
And then there are the others who'll say, 'No no no —
It's the ones after '74, they're the ones! —
Get into them ones and don't bother with the rest!'
   Why this unhealthy schism? —
It's because it was in 1974 that Philip K. Dick had the pink
   light experience —
Whether Philip K. Dick did in fact encounter the Almighty —
Or whether it was something else —
Sometimes he writes of it as 'being bathed in living
   knowledge' . . .
The title of that post-74 work 'VALIS', is an acronym for
   Vast Active Living Intelligence System —
And chum, I've got this: *The Selected Letters of Philip K.
   Dick 1974* —
i.e., only the letters that he wrote the year of the pink light —
And it's £39.95, and quite right – that'll keep the wankers off it —
If you're Philip K. Dickering, this one's probably a good start:
Divine Invasions – A Life of Philip K. Dick by Lawrence Sutin —
Lawrence Sutin's an American who knew Dick in the last
   few years of his life —
And wonderfully he flew over to be with us at the annual
   East London Dickheads Convention —
And it was Lawrence who told us about Philip K. Dick *and
   the snuff* —
Evidently Dick was into snuff in a big way —
(He was a big man, with a beard) —
And he'd be regaling the lads with new theories —
as to what the fuck had happened to him in 1974, u.s.w. —
And he'd have all these tins of snuff ranged in front of him —
about nine or ten tins in different flavours —
snuff comes in different flavours! —

And he'd be going from one tin of snuff to another —
amazing the guys —
And Lawrence described Dick as being 'covered in snizz' —
I'd never seen my hero in that light before —
Covered in snizz. Wow! —
And I thought, Well if I'm ever going to excite the seekers
    to anything like the degree that Dick has excited me, I've
    probably got to get into snuff —
I thought it'd be kinda nifty if after my death, people would say:
'Did you ever actually see him? Did you ever see Campbell?'
And they'd say, 'Yeah yeah, I did' —
'Wow, what was he like?' —
'Well, he was . . . covered in snizz!' —
And of course if you really want to get into anything, you
    discover it's just round the corner —
and been there for years —
In the newsagent Patel's they'd been grinding up snuff for
    years —
and they'd grind up any flavour you like —
I found that menthol, mentholated snuff was my chap —
Listen: throw away the fags! throw away the Havanas, boys! —
Snuff! —
That is the BIG ONE! —
And I was in my local, the Anchor and Hope*, demonstrating
    to Les the landlord the art of snuff-taking —
when into the bar came our local star: Buster Bloodvessel,
    leader of the Bad Manners pop group —
And Buster's like the Laughing Buddha on one side —
and like Boris Karloff in *Grip of the Strangler* on the other —
Buster entered the bar enantiodromically, and for humour he
    went:
'AAAAHHH **TCHOOOO**!' in my snuff tin —
Blasted all the snuff everywhere! —
'I'll have to get some more now!' (posing as amused) —

---

*See *Furtive Nudist* pp. 65–6, 79 and 81.

But not to worry —
because that day; Buster had this little run-around boy who
   was doing everything for him – any little errand – on a BMX
   bike —
And so I told the lad to go round to Patel's —
and to be sure to get it ground up with the menthol —
And I gave him the right money.

A long time later I learned this:
That the little lad had spent some of my money on comics,
   and bought some bubblegum —
so he got lightweight of snuff —
On the way back, I guess he was a wee bit worried about
   this —
So, passing a dried up dog turd of similar hue he snapped
   the tip off and crumbled it into the bag —
I just innocently funnelled it into my tin —
And then snuffled up a couple of pinches —
I said: 'Les, have you had an incontinent dog in here? —
I think a dog's shit somewhere . . .' —
'I can't smell anything,' says Les —
I said, 'Well clear your nose with this then' —
And he said: 'It's good stuff that! I've got it now' —
And Buster's drummer comes in, and sees Les and me sniffing
   around on our hands and knees —
He says: 'What are you guys doing down there?' —
Les said: 'There's a dog shit somewhere!' —
'I can't smell it,' says Drummer —
'Clear his nose, Ken,' says Les . . .

When I got home, I felt a bit Philip K. Dicky —
And you know how you go into the bathroom, to see if you're
    ill? —
I was looking in the mirror —
and I thought, No no – we're alright. There's Elsie, there's
    the Spanking Squire —
We're all present and correct —
And then I had a revelation —
Back to the pub: 'Buster! Boys! Look at my nose! —
Try and divorce my nose from the rest of my face! What
    does it remind you of?' —
And Buster said, 'Smugglers' coves! With 'orrible stalagmites!' —
'What?' I said. 'No no – not the nostrils —
Be looking more at the body of the nose . . .'
But they couldn't get anything —
I said, 'Look, is it not a naked lady from the rear? —
There's the cleavage of her buttocks at the end —
And there's her thighs – a wee bit spread —
And you can't see her hair because she's washing it.' —
And they got it —
'Yeah yeah. It's quite a turn on, your nose, as it happens' —
(There was tasteless humour about the pubes —
which has made me self-conscious about my nasal hair —
I trim the stuff every morning —
and keep the clippings in a jar.) —
Buster's drummer, he's got kids, and (giving me dolls' house
    sofa) he said, 'Here you are Ken! Something for her to sit
    on! Ah hah haahhh!' —
When I got home, I was doing my Stuart Pearce impressions:
'*A knife in the back . . . is not what we call . . . a normal
    death, CARSTAIRS!*' —
There was a knock at the door – it was Buster —
And Buster had had a vision. 'It's Cinderella, Ken!' he said.
    'It's a Cinderella fing!' —
I said, 'What is?' He said, 'Your nose is: – it's Cinderella
    and the slipper! —

What you've got to do, you've got to comb the land for her
   whose arse matches your nose —
and then *slip her one*!' —
'I've got a song coming on,' he said, and left.

It was just a silliness to begin with —
People would come round, get a bit pissed —
I'd get the Polaroid out: 'Will it be you my dear?' —
I don't think it would have gone any further than that —
if it hadn't been for the coming of Dick's *Exegesis* —
Philip K. Dick – a prolific man. He wrote forty novels before
   1974 —
then there was the pink light and he only wrote four* —
But he wasn't being lazy —
Every day he was at the typewriter —
often typing through the night —
But mostly this stuff wasn't for publication —
It was like letters —
but not letters *to* anybody —
Letters maybe to the very depths of himself —
And he called this stuff his *Exegesis* —
And when he died, he left behind about four million words
   in bundles and boxes —
and Lawrence Sutin had now read it all, and Lawrence sent me:
Selections from the Exegesis – the first published fragments
   of the legendary *Exegesis* of Dick† —
And Lawrence warned me that you couldn't get into this one
   unless you'd first read his selected significant terms at the
   back, the glossary —
'Otherwise you won't be able to make head or tail of it,' he said —

Valis, The Divine Invasion, The Transmigration of Timothy Archer, Radio Free Albemuth.
†*In Pursuit of Valis – Selections from the Exegesis* edited by Lawrence Sutin, published by Underwood-Miller, Novato, California 1991.

And that's where I found 'Enantiodromia' —

'*Enantriodromia*: the sudden transformation into an opposite form or tendency. The term was used by Heraclitus, but PKD [Dick] first became familiar with it through his reading of C.G. Jung . . .'

So there we are: I'm only the fourth person to use it, I guess — Heraclitus, then Jung, then Dick, then me — And on the next page is 'Pigspurt' — It says: '*Pigspurt*: see *Plasmate*' — Not an awfully difficult thing to do because *Plasmate* is the next word.

'*Plasmate*: Literally *living* knowledge. PKD often felt that he had bonded with it in 2-3-74,† and that, as a result, there dwelled within his psyche what seemed to be a *second* entirely other self . . . At times, Dick believed that the identity of this second self was the late James A. Pike . . .'

(Incidentally Bishop Pike, the heretical bishop of California who came to believe that Jesus was a mushroom) —

'. . . with whom PKD had been friends in the mid-1960s. At other times, he posited an early Christian named Thomas . . .'

blah blah blah – Here we go! —

'. . . Yet another identity posed by PKD was Pigspurt, a malevolent force that had filled him with fear and a craven attitude toward governmental authority; but it should be noted that Pigspurt was seldom mentioned – PKD rarely regarded this second self as malevolent. As for the plasmate itself, he most often regarded it as the living transmission of the Gnostic goddess Saint Sophia, Holy Wisdom. Another name coined by Dick for this Holy Wisdom was Firebright.'

*2-3-74 is Dick's shorthand term for his pink light experiences of February through March, 1974.

I thought, well one thing's for sure: I'm going to nick this
 word 'Enantiodromia' —
at that moment was born a nice little earner —
The Enantiodromic Approach to Drama! —
But it occurred to me, that maybe I ought to tart up my
 facets a bit, to go with the fancy prices —
Maybe it could be done under will? —
But I couldn't think that overnight I could transform inept
 vacant housewife Elsie into Saint Sophia the Gnostic Gnoddess
 of Holy Wisdom —
Maybe not into Saint Sophia, but what about Sophie – Sophie
 Firebright!? —
And the Squire? Perhaps Squire Pigspurt! *Spanking Squire
 Pigspurt*!! —
There was a knock at the door and it was Buster's
 drummer —
Buster's drummer had become more obsessed with my nose
 than I was —
he'd knocked up a little place for my nose lady, —

a box set (in fact made of an apple box) —
a miniature boudoir —
with dressing table and mirror —
and with my nose stuck in —
(and this I suggest was the achievement) —
it was more sexy than funny.

Pigspurt! 'twould be true to say that there was now a most
   decided nasal excitation to life! —
Sometimes I feared 'twas something worse: Nasal Infestation! —
That somewhere along the line, I had allowed into my nose
   some sort of daemonic urge —
That the daemon Pigspurt had taken up residence in my nose, —
and I was now to be led places, literally, by the nose —
Certainly it was something way beyond Stuart Pearce impressions
   that I was into now —
Sometimes blasphemous poetry would ring in the thing, like:

'Here come the Noz, the Noz of Nozareth
Also known as the Nozarene.
I say to one "Go!" and she goeth,
I say to another "Come!" and she cometh.
I say to another "Do this!" and she dothitheth it.'

(It's only right to warn you, that we've now reached the point in
the proceedings which Claire Armitstead of the *Guardian* found
'bemusingly unfunny'.)

THE ADVENTURES OF PIGSPURT

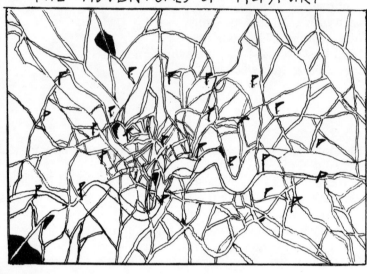

A map of London, and the pins stuck in it mark the points
of my major nasal adventures across the capital —
Of course, I would argue it to myself in this way: that it
was research —
That I was researching what would undoubtedly become a
British classic erotic nasal novel —
Where is such a thing? —
The French threw down the gauntlet with *Cyrano de Bergerac
(Version Bleu)* —
The Italians replied with *Pornochio* —
Ours will be: *The Adventures of Pigspurt* —
And what, pray, will we find in those pages? —
Well, let's just have a look at some of the research, shall we? —
Location 14: Finsbury Park – the actual park —

I had on my flying helmet, my usual headgear for a night
on the snout —
There's a not unpleasant café in Finsbury Park – certainly
the coffee's drinkable —
and in there I got into pleasant chat with a woman in her
mid-thirties —
À propos of not a lot, I said: 'Have a look at my nose —
Does it make you think of anything?' —
Well no, it just looked like a nose to her —
So I pointed out the secret of it: the cleavage and the thighs
and wotnot —
She was amused by the concept —
So I went out to the car and I brought in the Boudoir Box —
She went hysterical —
And then I told her about my scheme —
that I was combing the land for her whose arse matched my
nose —
And she was up for it! —
Wheeeeeeeeeeeeeeee! —
And we were round the back of the toilets —
with the Polaroid! —
Well, one thing led to another —
And in the middle of the another, I thought:
I know the name for this —
this is cunninasus! —
Coitus Proboscidalis!! —
And then with her legs akimbo, like the flesh wings of an
aircraft, and me in my Biggles hat —
Fundamental orifice, my intercom! —
And I suddenly started broadcasting more of my poem up it:

'Here comes the Schnozz,
the Schnozz of Schnozzareth,
Also known as the Schnozzarene . . .'

And then I was subject to a roaring of form, —
proboscidoidal extension! —
then (actual or illusory, I know not) ejaculation! —
Not that I snotted up her —
more that a pinnacle blowhole had been miraculously and
    momentarily formed for the occasion —
As I pulled out, I thought: I hope I haven't made her preg-
    nant —
and she'll give birth to a bogey baby —
I looked up and there was the Park Keeper —
'How's Alf?' he said.

Location 7 is of interest I think. Location 7 was a Malay
    lady who ended all her sentences with 'innit' – ('n' it?) —
What I mean is, invariably and ludicrously, —
e.g: 'I like your hat, do you want a cup of tea, innit?' —
Sometimes she'd mint Zen koans: 'Can you pass the sugar,
    innit?' —
Something amazing could occasion the further addition of 'nell'
    – [Nell: poss. abbr. 'Fucking Hell'] —
as: '. . . she snorted it *all* up and got completely out of it,
    innit, nell!' —
And so I called her 'Innit Nell' —
Anyway, regarding this cunninasus stunt, she declared herself
    to be 'Really inuit, innit' —
Really Inuit! —
I said, 'So you're really Inuit Nell? —
You're Inuit Nell! Eskimo Nell!!' —
She didn't get it – ('I don't get it, innit,' she said) —
But she wanted me to go along to this club she knew —
She thought that some of the members of the club might
    be 'inuit' too —
She warned me that there was a strict dress code at the club —

I said, 'Well you can count me out if you like. I don't like
    going to places where they force you into a dickie-bow tie
    and all that' —
But that wasn't her meaning, no no. 'Just put your Biggles
    hat on, innit!' —
Anyway, this club is just off the Charing Cross Road, round
    the back of Foyles, and it only meets on a Monday —
and it's called the Scented Crowbar —
They let me in, but once inside I felt overdressed in my flying
    helmet —
The first guys who riveted one's gaze were old fat men —
One of them looked like my old Latin master —
And all they'd got on . . . —
what they must have done is, they must have each removed
    the cylindrical core from a toilet roll, then wrapped them
    round with gaffer tape, and then stuck their plonkers in –
    tied them up round the back, and shoved a few daffodils up
    their bums —
There were fifty-year-old cubs there, with a sort of Mrs Denn
    cub-mistress type, ready to slipper them round the back of
    the legs if they got out of order —
And then there were bishops there —
and Venuses in Furs —
But in the main the ladies of the Scented Crowbar adopt
    this mode: leotards cut high, and fishnet stockings, very
    high-heeled shoes, bunched up Charlie Chesters, and a little
    'floggaroo' tucked under the arm —
This berky chap in studded codpiece comes up and says: 'How's
    Alf?' —
I tell him he's all right —
'Oh look!' says my new chum who did film reviewing for
    Time Out, 'See him over there?' —
Him over there is what had looked to be mini-skirted starlet —
'See him? He's the Head of the Art Department of the Romford
    Comprehensive —
And he's married to that fat dominatrix over there —

We didn't half have some fun over their place last week —
We'd got the block and tackle out, and we'd hoisted Ted
     up to the ceiling, —
(Where's Ted? – You'll meet Ted!) —
and he was all gagged and bound, just his arse hanging out
     waiting for his wallops —
And then somebody there actually knew what the Footsie 100
     Index is, and we got so interested in that, that we forgot about
     Ted!' —
The bar prices in there were really quite reasonable —
And there was disco music playing —
You'd get toilet-roll beplonkered old Latin masters dancing
     with bishops, and some fellow who'd come as
     Frank Bough —
And I thought, What harm in it? It's just people who like
     to dress up . . . —
But then the music changed —
The disco music's gone, and now there's unhealthy church
     music playing —
of an order to separate the Bishops from the boys —
And onto the stage was trolleyed a mighty set of mediaeval
     stocks —
And the first up onto the stage was the Head of the Art
     Department of the Romford Comprehensive —
He offers his hands and head to the stocks —
And he's padlocked in by a beefy dominatrix lady —
Now joined by a partner —
they yank down his fatuous knicks —
and it's going to be canes first. —
If you went to a school where they practised corporal punishment,
     when someone's getting it, you always do one thing:
You count! —
Whack! goes the first lady, Whack! the second: Two —
Three! ... Four! ... Five! ..... Eight! .... Eighteen! ....
     Twenty-five!
Phorr! —

And then fresh ladies are called for —
High cut leotards and little 'floggaroos'! —
the cat-o-nineteen tails —
And they whisk him with the cat-o-nineteen tails for another
    twenty-five —
And again fresh ladies called for! —
I don't know where they get these things from: like over-sized
    table tennis bats (I guess you apply to a short-sighted ping-
    pong club) —
Anyway, when you've got one of these things, you screw wicked
    studs in it —
And he gets another twenty-five with the studded ping-pong
    bat —
Then he's let out, and up comes a toilet-roll beplonkered Latin
    master to get his regulation seventy-five! —
I count five of them through the stocks and by that time,
    I thought, God I've got to have a piss! —
The thing is, I'd put off going to the Gents in this place —
I thought it might be a bit chummy for my taste —
But I've got to go now! —
And it was like a torture chamber in there! —
There were guys had been craned right up to the ceiling,
    all gagged and chained —
There's this bloke up on the ceiling, all zipped up in a backwards
    helmet —
and he says: 'If you just want to have a pee, go in the Ladies' —
There's a real beefy pair of ladies in the Ladies —
Fishnet stockings? —
They'd be happier in sprout bags —
Anyway, they were fixing up thumb screws and horse whips for
    later in the evening, and I thought, I'm not getting it out in
    here! —
And the main event in the ballroom now was a free-for-all —
About nineteen old gentlemen's arses – bared and thrust into
    the podium – and nine or ten of these fine ladies walloping,
    and lashing round them with whips and bats —

And I thought, They must have filthy Gods these guys! —
And then they looked like so many sick old noses to me,
  these arses —
A nasal nightmare! —
And suddenly I thought NO – I'VE GOTTA GET OUT! —
And I had a piss in the side doorway of Foyles.

Now this was the odd thing: coming up Charing Cross Road —
(and usually I can tell the difference between a hallucination
  and a thing, and this was definitely a thing) —
was a NOSE —
or rather somebody in a nose outfit —
You could see his little feet coming through the nostrils of
  his nose costume —
I thought, Wow! What club's he been to?

When I got home from the Scented Crowbar, the front door
  was swinging wide open and there was no one in —
I'd been burgled —
They'd taken the television set, they'd taken the video
  recorder —
they left me the remote —
(and a whoopsie on the carpet) —
and they'd taken the word processor (sort of good news that) —
BUT they'd taken a load of my papers – including the *Pigspurt
  Diaries*.

In Homerton Police Station, the duty officer, when there was
   no one around, said: 'If you take my advice Mr Campbell,
   you'll leave the area, otherwise you'll wind up dead one night
   – or worse. Not everyone here is your friend' —
And he concluded by shuffling his papers – (a bit of biz he'd
   learnt off ITN) —
When I got back home it seemed to me that I owned too
   much stuff —
I got the bin bags out, and I thought: I don't need this any
   more, I don't need these, and I don't want anyone finding
   that! —
And then through the 'postofis letahol' came a leaflet —
from the Victims of Burglary Support Group —

   Dear Victim of Burglary,
   You are probably doing one or other of these things now: . . .

And one of them was: stuffing all your gear in bin bags
   to chuck out —
And then a phone call from the Victims of Burglary Support
   Group —
Would I like one of them to come and chat with me? —
Have a sit with me? —
Well . . . No. NO! —
I was beginning to put two and two together in a rather sinister
   way —
I thought the odds were that it was the cops —
It was the cops, obviously, who'd come in and thieved all
   my gear! —
And the Victims of Burglary Support Group? —
They're just part of the evil machinery —
They just want to grind you down, and squeeze a bit more
   information out of you —
So I said: 'No no, don't worry about me. I'm fine thank
   you' —
But I carried on throwing my stuff out —

But then the bin men, instead of properly slinging my stuff
in the back of the cart —
They took my stuff in with them —
Into the driver's cab . . . —
(Incidentally, I found that with the TV remote I could make
the neighbour's cat run up the curtains) —
Anyway, I wrote a stern letter to whoever was now in charge
of investigating my garbage:

Dear Sir/Madam,
Why don't you just come out into the open!? Tell me what
you want instead of this rather childish James Bond
routine.

And I posted the letter into my dustbin.

I tell you one thing, I'd hung up my spurting helmet for good
and all now —
And any time I was away from home, I'd take the opportunity
to write myself a letter —
in disguised handwriting, on a borrowed typewriter, as if from
a friend or a relative —
And they'd heard about the nonsense I'd got into —
Listen, we all know this don't we: All men of a certain age
. . . they get into some nonsense or other —
And they'd all heard about my recent silliness and they were
just *so pleased* that I'd got through it without any need for
psychiatric help . . . —
It was just so I could receive these things – and screw them
up and put them in my bin —
To settle things —
But then Buster Bloodvessel and the whole buggering band
burst in —

Buster had now written the Song of my Nose —
'**** Nose!' —
And he was going to be launching it that night in the George
  Robey pub in Finsbury Park —
There was no oddsing it: I was picked up bodily by the band
  and carried out in some sort of triumph to the blue Transit
  and off to the George Robey —
Amazing gig – but then comes the moment I'd been dreading —
and the spotlight fingers the hall and finds me – and Buster
  points my nose out to the world!
Its thighs, its pubes and how it's inspired this next song:

But while they were playing I saw it! —
If such a thing does exist I saw it! —
The womanly posterior which matches my nose! —
Yes, yes, my darling, mmm, YARCHH!! —
Arghhh! —
Oh no! My nose in three and blood everywhere —
The fiancé of the phenomenon had read my mind —
And I was carted out and off to Homerton Hospital.

The specialist in Homerton said, 'Well it's a mess. You're
   going to need rhinoplasty' —
Rhinoplasty? Apparently a word simply meaning to fix up your
   nose —
'But,' he said, 'You can have it done like anything you like
   now' —
And when he said that, there was this chunky little nurse
   called Tracy who was filling in some sort of medical thing,
   bending down, and indicating her chummy buttocks; I said,
   'Can I have it done like that?' —
And she was really quite tickled by that, Tracy was —
and we became quite good friends —
(just friends – there was nothing nasal about this) —
When they let me out of the hospital, Tracy said that her
   mother wanted to meet me —
Listen, I think if you've got a mother like Tracy's you should
   give a bit more warning than she gave —
Tracy's really quite short, but her mother Olive is really quite
   tall —
Olive embraced me warmly, kissed me on both cheeks and
   said (this is our first meeting!): 'When you go to Australia,
   go to Perth as well as Sydney, but you're thinking of going
   to Canada first, aren't you dear? —
Why am I getting doughnuts?' —
She said: 'You've been very lazy about the Caribbean, haven't
   you dear?' —
I said, 'Well I don't ever think about it' —
'What a shame,' she said. 'I can see you on the island of
   Curacao, I can see you on Surinam, I can see you in Guyana —
When you go to Guyana ring this telephone number: Georgetown
   72629 —

But you've got other islands in mind at the moment, haven't
   you dear? —
Six pigs from happiness – Is that a song? And what did
   happen to David?' —
I said, 'Look, what is this?' —
She said, 'Well, I don't know where I get anything from dear;
   why – was it any help to you?'

Anyway, I rather got into Tracy's mum Olive —
Olive loved a tipple —
(Tipple! Some nights we *swam* together) —
Olive took a great deal of interest in the figurines —
It was Olive's opinion that the figurines represented an attempt
   at communication by the late Captain Charlie Charrington —
She said, 'The first one you found was which dear?' —
'The Dog-dragon,' I told her —
'And what was the first thing you thought of?' —
'I saw the face of Captain Charlie Charrington' —
She said, 'Well there you are dear, that's the Captain saying:
   "Dear Kenneth, this is your Captain speaking" —
And then you found the Legs —
Is there anything wrong with your legs, dear?' —
'Well, I have to click my hip every now and then' —
She said, 'Well maybe you should be clicking it more, dear
   – I don't know —
But,' she said, 'it's really clear what the Captain's saying with
   the Shrieking Monk —
What he's saying is: "I have things of theological importance
   for you, but I am gagged."
You must seek to remove the Captain's gag, dear —
and you'll do that by way of your legs, no doubt —
Maybe you've got to go on a hiking holiday, I don't know —
Or maybe you've got to "consider legness" —

Drape your legs, perhaps? *Who's Sophie?'* —
'Where did you get Sophie from?'
'From your map dear!' —
She took a ball of knitting wool out of her bag —
(in trance, she smirks, Olive) —
and with the wool she joined up my nasal adventure flags
   in such a way that they spelled out:

THE ADVENTURES OF PIGSPURT

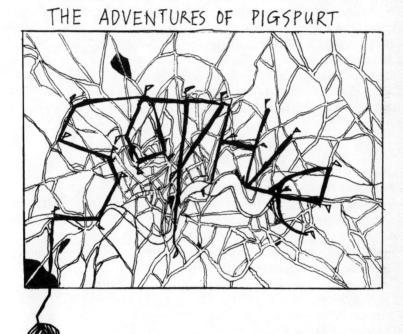

I found myself making a full confession of everything to Olive —
Olive said, 'I think it's all very clear, isn't it dear? —

Everything is telling you that it's time now to soft-pedal on this
rather alarming side of your personality, the Squire Pigspurt
side, your Spanker, and time now to be stressing your softer,
your Sophie side' —
And Olive had the goodness now whenever she came round
to see me, always to sit to the right of me – to draw out
my Sophieness —
And then one evening, she said:
'A shop has just come in dear; it's round the back of Euston
station; it's in a road that begins with E; and it's next door
to the bookies, this shop; —
you'll think it's a television repair shop —
Go in there, dear —
There's a lady in there and she's something of a healer and
she may be able to help you, dear —
Tell her that you're having spiritual counselling.'

Well, I think the road referred to is Eversholt Street —
And next-door to the bookmakers is not a television repair
shop —
But there's a sign in the window saying: TV Wear —
You can't see in through the windows, they're black – opaque —
the name of this shop is Transformation —
I can't speak too highly of the staff of Transformation —
The ladies who serve and advise are real ladies —
(I'm sure they are . . . yes, they are) —
They pointed me towards the free coffee —
Free coffee in Transformation —
And I browsed around their wares —
Eventually finding myself in easy conversation with a lady whose
name tag informed us she was S. Heila ('Healer?') —
I said, 'I don't know what I'm doing here at all, actually —
I'm having spiritual counselling, and it is true that I'm meant

to be bringing out my feminine side a bit more, but I hadn't
thought I was meant to go tarting around the town!' —
S. Heila said: 'No no, you're having spiritual counselling. I
understand —
Has there been a name given to your female side yet?' —
I said, 'Yes, well there has, I suppose, yes: Sophie. Sophie
Firebright' —
'So,' she said, 'Sophie would be like an older woman who's
had all her babies?' —
'Yes,' I said, 'I suppose she would.' —
'She sounds to me, your Sophie, as if she's an environmental
lady —
Have a look at this – this is an environmental top' —
(handing me a cream blouse with built on green scarf) —
'What makes it environmental?' —
'I don't know really,' she said, 'but Greenpeace came in and
bought six.' —
She showed me a black skirt which apparently went very nicely
with the environmental tops —
And then she put a wig on me —
'to help me towards my Sophie' —
I said, 'S. Heila? What does the S stand for?' —
'Sheila,' she said —
'Sheila Heila?!' —
'No no no,' she said. 'There was a glitch in the machine when
it stamped it out —
It should just say "Sheila"' —
She said, 'So you're not going to be wearing any of this stuff
out and about then?' —
'No,' I said, 'absolutely not! I can only suppose that perhaps
I'm meant to sit about in it during my spiritual counselling
sessions' —
'In that case,' she said, 'I should be thinking about buying
a set of these —
If the object of the exercise is to make a visual impression on
other people, well, you can put what you like in your bra —

But if it's for *you* – these are the answer —
These are really quite weightier than you'd suppose, hold them,
    go on —' —
They were a mixture of medical and naughty —
Surprisingly weighty —
and CHEEKY! with a life of their own —
I would compare the experience with that of handling wet
    ferrets —
I went slightly hysterical in the grip muscles —
'You glue them to your chest, and you actually will get the
    feel – the swing and wotnot, of real bosoms.' —
But this stuff isn't cheap —
The environmental top is £39.99, —
£29.99 for the skirt that goes nicely with it, —
£59.99 for the wig; bra £19.99; shoes £49.99 —
But silicon bosoms range from £99 a pair to £350! —
And there was no point in me thinking I could get away
    with £99 ones either —
A fellow of my build would get hardly any benefit at all —
No swing or wotnot from those —
I'd have to start thinking from £175, and it's not going to
    stop there because then I'm going to need the Dow Corning
    Medical Adhesive at £29.99 a pot to stick them on —
and Dow Corning Medical Adhesive Remover at £24.95 a bottle
    to get them off —
And then you need the blue stuff to rub in after you've had
    all this stuff on —
This is insanity, I thought. I haven't got that sort of money
    anyway!

But what's a Barclaycard for?

When I got it home, I hid it until Olive came round —
And I said, 'Olive! – "television repair shop"!' —
She was quite amused, and said: 'Come along then dear, let's
    see you in your Sophies' —
'There's a revolution due in ladies' blouse buttons, isn't there?'
    I said to Olive, donning the gear —
'That's not really a button, and neither's that really a buttonhole!
    Fffiddle fiddle fiddle!' —
'That's the whole point dear,' said Olive. 'That's the spiritual
    worth of this exercise: to calm you down' —
And it was true, only with a genuine inner serenity could
    I cope with my blouse buttons —
Anyway I got it all on me, and it was quite amusing for
    a minute or two —
And then – and I really don't know how this happened, but
    there we were having ever such a nice chat like us ladies
    who've had all our babies do have —
And this became the form of things – when Olive popped
    round, if I was alone and not expecting company, she'd say:
    'Just slip into your Sophies, dear' —
I recall such very pleasant tender times —
But then she wanted me to go further —
To go out in my Sophies —
I said, 'No no no no no! There's absolutely no point in going
    out in it —
It's just pleasant what we do, I love it like this —' —
But one Wednesday evening she said: 'Come on dear, let's
    just go along to the Spiritualist Church —
It's healing night tonight; not many people go; nobody will
    pay you any attention in any case —
Where's your spirit of adventure, Sophie?' —
The Spiritualist Church is only half a mile away —

but that's quite far enough in high heels —
Stamford Hill —
I'm talking about that one with the big spire —
  and that winged cow on it —
Just a small congregation, —
no more than fifteen people —
But they'd gone to a lot of trouble with the candles business —
candles all over the place, and a fellow there playing the organ
  with warts —
I sat towards the back —
In the congregation was this elderly Caribbean lady, her shoulders
  hunched with age —
But it was her white beret which singled her out for my atten-
  tion —
I always spot out people wearing berets, and that's because
  of my mate of some years ago, Chris Langham —
Langham was always obsessed with the notion that he'd never
  do anything so wonderful that his name would live forever —
He reckoned if you wanted your name to live forever, you'd
  got to find some common or garden object which hadn't been
  named yet, and then give it your name —
Just before Christmas one year, he summoned everyone he
  knew to this hall —
Eventually he came out in front of us wearing only a little
  black beret —
And he pointed to the little whisp thing on the top, and said: —
'Ladies and Gentlemen: a langham!' —
We all helped Christopher out that year —
We bought everyone we knew berets for Christmas, so we
  could go into Harrods (etc.) demanding: 'A beret please.
  With a particularly chunky langham!' —
And that's what the elderly Caribbean lady had —
(her name was Ethel incidentally) —
a beret with a particularly chunky langham.

Of course it became a little bit regular, this popping along
  on a Wednesday to the healing with Olive —
On the fifth occasion, actually sixth, no fifth – Ethel wasn't
  there —
And when we came out, Olive said: 'I think we should go
  and call on Ethel dear.' —
I said, 'Well you can count me out, I'm going home!' —
'Come along dear, she's a very infirm and elderly lady; now
  come along' —
Ethel lived in those flats for old women round the back of
  Safeways and she was in bed in her beret —
Her old legs didn't work any more —
And Olive said: 'You know Sophie don't you? Sophie
  Firebright?' —
And then she said: *'Sophie does healing'* —
I went hot then cold and then had the feeling I was not
  the owner of my body —
(that I'd been renting it, maybe) —
And this is what I heard bursting from my lips:
'Mi bagaff hasmali, Ma bagaff himani, Ani lo yudiah haloutz
ma kazi —
Who's on the left-wing, What's on the right-wing, I Don't
  Know is centre forward, Ethel —
Im fulugud dei. Im fulugud dei blong yumitufala pushem lilfala
salwata wanae —
insaed postofis letahol blong praefala pasta —
talim – 'ski aelan twinki twink plantifala ia!'' —
And she was looking up at me – impressed, trusting —
And in demi-trance, I picked up the scissors and snipped off
  her langham —
And I passed her hatpin through the chunk of the langham
  making a simple crucifix which I pinned on her —

And I said, 'No pies —
No pies, there's no pies for you, Ethel – there's going to
   be NO PIES for you when you get Up There.'
And I kept repeating, 'No pies . . . No pies,' until I had
   tears streaming down my face —
'No pies, no pies. No pies, Ethel, unless you get up and
   give us a little walk around the room' —
And I was massaging her old legs now '. . . no pies . . .' —
and so was Olive '. . . no pies . . .' —
Olive was now singing her all-purpose interdenominational
   hymn —
'No pies, tra-la-la' —
And we got Ethel up, and we gave her a little trot round
   the room —
And we laid her back to bed and I said: 'Ani rotzah lekuleff
   tapuzeem!' —
'We ladies must peel oranges.' —
When we got out, Olive was hysterical —
She said; 'I think you've got the gift dear!' —
And when we got back, we polished off a whole bottle of
   Jamesons —
Olive went flakey on the sofa and had to stay the night —
The next week, Olive wasn't around —
Sometimes she had Spiritualist duties in Stoke-on-Trent or
   Iceland —
I think it was Stoke that week —
But it was Wednesday evening . . .
I thought: Well, I think I'm up to going to the healing
   on my own now —
So I put me Sophies on and popped off to the church.

And it was fine —
But Ethel wasn't there —

I thought, I know what Olive would like me to do; she'd
   like me to pop in on Ethel, make sure she's all right —
So I did; I popped in there, and Ethel was really much
   improved —
She was up and about —
She simply wasn't well enough to go to the healing —
She was reminiscing about her childhood in Guyana –
   GuyANNA, she called it —
And as she was remembering her girlhood chums —
I saw what a beautiful woman she'd once been —
And I rather felt an attack of the Pigspurts coming upon
   me —
She was fiddling around in the sink —
And I came up behind her, and I said: 'Ethel?'
She turned round – and I said:
'. . . Excuse me. There is something I must do!' —
And I got out of there —
Fled, like I was being pursued —
Cinderella at one minute to midnight! —
And as soon as I got in, I was throwing my gear off —
Bugger it! I thought. I've run out of blue stuff! —
And I was stuffing away my kit —
I thought, They're coming for me! —
They're coming for me tonight! —
But even so, there was to be a moment where I halted
   my disrobing —
I was dropping the skirt, when I stopped —
the skirt still draped halfway down my legs —
my legs look for all the world like the legs of the figurine! —
And in looking across to the Pair of Legs on the mantelpiece,
I catch sight of my own bare bum in the mirror —
UH HAHH! HA-HAHHH!! UH HA!!! HA! HAHHH!!!!
And I realized, *'t was my own arse I sought*! —
UH HAHH! HA-HAHHH!! UH HA!!! HA-HAHHH!!!!!
I thought, What's that noise? —
UH HAHH! UH-HAHHH!! UH HA!!! HA-HAHHH!!!!

And I realized: It's me. IT'S ME! I'm laughing like the
   Bishop of Colchester! —
It's an ingenious way of laughing that actually, because there
   comes a point when you can't remember what you were
   laughing at —
You're just laughing because your last laugh was so *deranged*!
There comes a point though, where it dies down —
And you remember I mentioned before about my being subject
   to attacks of paralysis?
'entropy of the bone marrow' —
It was setting in that night —
and there was a musty smell to the place —
And shuffling movements —
And I'd turn round but I couldn't see what was doing it —
Then I felt there to be a challenge in the air —
And I was fighting to put it into words —
And I was reaching into the unthinkable —
The unspeakable —
But maybe, if I attempted performance of the unperformable
   I might **unscrew the inscrutable!** —
If I only dared —
If I could only persuade myself to —
GO UP MY OWN ARSEHOLE!

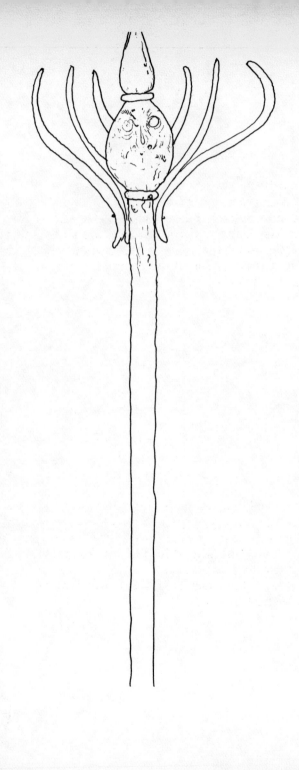

I could still see the room —
but hazily —
But then I was aware I was not alone! —
That I had a bearded visitor! —
'In the most unlikely place, Kenneth' He said —
'Just as Mrs Denn told you. In fact Mrs Denn and Miss
   O'Halloran hit the concept round about plumb centre' —
And He was going round the room, —
looking for clues! —
but with an *authority* —
I saw now how the business might be attempted without getting
   a laugh —
'Omniae viae ad Deum ducent!' He said; 'All paths lead
   to God. But some are quicker than others —
Your quick way was up your own arse *and you were born
   with the clue*!' —
I said, 'But I had my nose fixed; I had rhinoplasty —
I had it made to look like Tracy's . . .' —
'Yes yes,' He said. 'But we in our wisdom afflicted you with
   haemorrhoids! —
Walking that way, the tension and wotnot, soon got your
   bum back in nasal harmony! . . . —
Heaven and Hell, Kenneth, are basically the same place —
The good go to a good part of it, the bad go to a bad part of
   it, the fairly nice go to a fairly nice eternal picnic in a sort of
   park; louts lout around in the lout compound —
**but *comedians sit with me*! —
Current favourites: Benny Hill, Eric Morecambe, and the Bishop
   of Colchester —

b'doom   b'doom   b'doom   b'doom

we have to keep sending the Grim Reaper down for cubs
   for him though! —
You see, they only think in these extreme forms of Heaven
   and Hell because of the absurdly enantiodromic nature of
   my set up here' —
I said: 'Wow, and that's it for all eternity then, is it, sir?' —
'That's it until I blow the whistle, dear boy,' He said —
'What happens then, sir?' —
'Well,' He said, 'I was thinking of blowing it quite shortly
   as a matter of fact —
Maybe next February or March —
After all, it's about time to get stuck in to some of that
   stuff that I let slip to Saint John the Divine —
Beasts with hundreds of eyes before and behind —
and the parting of the heavens, and the moving of the mountains,
   and the islands out of their places . . . —
But how tickled I am,' He said —
'How tickled I am that you found your way up to me so that
   we can have this farewell theophany before the Big Spring
   Clean —
You know, Kenneth, this hint of appalling pattern that you
   contrive to get in your stories? —
That is an intimation of the Divine —' —
'Wow,' I said. 'Is it really? But to do that I have to bend
   the truth a bit, you know —
Sometimes I put things out of their real order —
Sometimes I just invent things' —
'They are nonetheless intimations of the Divine!' He said —
'Yes,' I said, 'but don't I get my "God" a little bit grubby? –

and thus I'll get shunted to a less salubrious part of Heaven
   – ? —' —
'Oh very much so!' said the Lord —
'But that doesn't sound quite fair to me then!' I said —
'So what is this Creation of yours then? A cock-up? A conspiracy?
   What is it?' —
'It is both!' said the Lord. 'Yours is an enantiodromic world —
But I disguised it —
But Heraclitus tumbled it —
So did Carl Gustav Jung and your Dick —
But all that was manageable —
But then, Kenneth, you started your Enantiodromic Two-Faced
   Acting Workshop Class Thingies —
Your Enantiodromic Two-Faced Acting Workshop Class
   Thingies are as much responsible for the need for a
   spring clean here as anything else —
If any of that stuff had got generally known, you would
   have unravelled the whole fabric —
The basic set-up here, humanitywise, is this:
The big guys get to whang between exciting extremes while
   the wankers hide in caves' —
I said, 'Am I to take it then, that your Commandments
   are to be seen as challenges?' —
'Oh very much so!' said the Lord. 'The Commandments!? —
The Commandments are only there to keep the berks in
   some sort of order! —
And out of the hair of the men of vision! —
   Churchill! . . . Maxwell! . . . the Mongol Hordes! . . . David
   DeNil! . . .' —
I was confused —
'I am hinge point,' He explained. 'Herman Melville wrote of
   me:

"Yea and nay, each hath his say,
But God,
He keeps to the middle way." —

I am balance and Satan is all around infinitely —
But I am infinity, and I try everything infinitely —' —
And the Lord had now picked up my Philip K. Dick Society
    Pamphlet:
'If you find this world bad, you should see some of the others,'
He read and nodded —
'Thus anything anywhere at any one moment is absurd —
The fragmentation being infinite —
But viewed *as a whole*, which is a perspective peculiarly mine,
    it is a pattern of full and infinite richness —' —
And the Lord had now picked up my *Ken Dodd: Laughter
    and Tears* by Gus Smith —
I said, 'We've met before, haven't we?'
'Mm hmm,' said the Lord —
'No, what I mean is, you've *appeared* to me before —' —
And I was racking through my thoughts . . . —
I said, 'I know! It was you who barged into my dream and told
    me to tell David DeNil he'd got to go and see every live show
    that Ken Dodd gave for a year!' —
'Oh yes I love Doddy!' said the Lord. 'Live!' He qualified —
'I trust you approved of my intervention in his tax affairs?' —
'Oh yes certainly,' I said. —
'I thought I'd be sussed there!' said God —
'So,' I said. 'When Ken Dodd told David DeNil he was
    going to Efaté in the New Hebrides . . . —' —
'Oh that was me speaking through him!' said God —
'Wow, so Ken Dodd's pretty important in the current scheme
    of things then?' —
'Oh you always knew that!' said God, —
'Yes,' I said. 'But I tell you what I'm still foxed over: what's
    the link then between Ken Dodd and the Solomon Islands?' —
'Here's one!' said the Lord, turning to page 83 of the Gus
    Smith book . . .
'Ooh look!' said God. 'You've even underlined it.' —
(This is Doddy talking directly to Gus, and he's saying:)

*'I would definitely count myself as an expert on the subject of what turns a man on. After all, I'm a professor of tickleology. But let's take the sensual bits first. With a man, certain parts of a lady have definite appeal. Some are leg men, calf men, ankle or cheek men. **I'm an upper arm and shoulder man, that's definitely one of the nicest bits.**'*

UH HAHH! HA-HAHHH!! UH HA!!! HA-HAHHH!!!!
'So Ken Dodd was a Solomon Islander in a previous life!' —
'Don't get into all that,' said God. 'Previous lives and wotnot! —
You're not equipped to deal with what's really going on!' —
'But something like that maybe,' I said —
God was now frigging about with my new VCR. 'Show
 me how this works!' He said —
'Actually' I said, 'I only know how to play a video on it' —
'Oh no!' He said. 'You can set these things up to record
 programmes up to a year ahead!' —
'Yes I know,' I said, 'but I've been busy. But I tell you
 what's worrying me,' I said —
'This beast with all the eyes before and behind and the mountains
 and islands moving out of their places Revelation business —
Is there anything any of us can do about that?' —
The Lord was poring over the Mitsubishi VCR instruction
 booklet —
'This manual is incomprehensible!' declared the Lord. 'In all
 the languages!' —
'Except Japanese,' I said.
'No it's complete garbage in Japanese!' – said God —
'Sorry – what? The parting of the heavens and the great
 pooof!? No, there's nothing that can be done about that,'
 He said, 'No! —
'Tis writ! —
Well,' He said. 'Look; I would hold it off *only* . . . if could
 be found a man of good heart who would undertake to go
 and see every live show Ken Dodd gives for a year' —

'Well,' I said, 'I'm afraid I don't believe in you any more sir —
I don't even *suppose* in you any more —
That really is too absurd —' —
'I AM INFINITELY ABSURD!' said the Lord —
His words slippered the backs of my legs and I subsided
   on my knees —
'Sir,' I said. 'sir! Will I ever be forgiven for my snouting,
   for my days of Pigspurting?' —
'*Your days of Pigspurting*?' said the Lord, cruelly impersonating
   my accent —
'What's your problem boy? You never intruded, did you? —
You were always invited up, weren't you?' He said —
'You charmed them with your Boudoir Box and wotnot! —
and there was nothing daemonic about that!' He said —
'He whom you thought of as Pigspurt, that was you! —
You allowed your own repressed self to manifest! —
You must face it Kenneth: you are a *funny* fucker! —
Recall if you will any of the reactions of your various partners
   to your cunnisneezus . . .?' —
'Well,' I said, 'hysteria, tittering' —
'Exactly so!' said the Lord. 'You was a Professor of
   Tickleology —
Did you know, the Solomon Islanders were into cunnisneezus
   from the dawning of mankind? —
Why do you think they wear those feathers in their noses? —
But if I may', He said, 'I'd like to hint this: when you
   got that old lady up and walking I WAS NOT THERE! —
What would you make of that statement, Kenneth?' —
I said, 'What, you mean there was merely angelic involvement?
   . . . Daemonic?' —
'THAT WAS PIGSPURT!' He said 'How's Alf?' —
And He disappeared miraculously through the wall.

I said. 'Oy! Come back! Get back in here! You weren't God!' —
'You summoned, Kenneth?' (Bearded Gent halfway through
   the wall) —
'Take off the beard!' I said —
. . . the beard came off easily —
He now stepped fully into the room —
And a curly-brimmed bowler appeared on his head —
'Captain!' I said —
'Thanks for looking after Dee,' he said —
'I just wrote to her a few times, and went to see her once,' I said.
'All it takes,' said the Captain —
'Now listen,' he said. 'That wasn't a theophany —
I was posing as God —
Celestial espionage – but even that's a cover —
I'm part of a bunch who are heretically attached to mankind
   and life as you know it —
We love you Life! But like an old dog —
And it's time now, to put Life out of its misery —
You don't want Johnny Div's Revelations here —
So we're going for a final ingression of novelty; implosion of
   the entire multi-dimensional continuum of space and time; the
   megamacrocosmos to go down the plughole as the hyperspatial
   vacuum fluctuations of paired particles (i.e., your universe)
   collides with its own ghost image after billions of years of
   separation —
Why do they all have these irrational feelings of loss? —
Because **nothing** is the natural state. **Something** is perversion:
In order to create chronological matter out of the Nothing
   Nowhere, the Great Perverter had to separate forwards from
   backwards, positive from negative, **matter from antimatter** —
And me and the crew think we can bring the two together
   and engineer an Apocatastasis —
Every subatomic particle (except photons) will cancel each
   other out, the entire Universe quietly disappearing up its
   own bumhole —
Merely the whimper that Tommy Eliot spoke of —

a little Wh-ha-hoo! —
and only photons will exist, and we will have liberated the
    Universe of Light from the Black Iron Prison of Matter! —
And all Life will find itself walking up the path of the Promised
    Garden —
This time (we trust) demanding full inclusion in the plans
    for Phase Two!'

'Phorr,' I said, then 'Wow! Look, I'm just talking off the top
    of my head at the moment, but this is how it sounds to me
    on this side of the veil:
I've got a little daughter – she's not so little any more, she's 14 —
    and I really looked after her —
not like you just seeing her four times in a lifetime! —
And I'd really like her to live on, mine. I want her to live on! —
I want her to live on and face it! Whatever it's going to be! —
The Revelations or what the fuck —
Without, actually, thank you, sir, your kindness of this Apocat-
    astasis' —
'Then book your tickets for Ken Dodd!' he said —
'The first messages will come through on the 13th of March
    1993 during the "What a beautiful day" sequence' —
I said, 'First or second house?' —
'Second – but only if you see the first' —
'Yeah,' I said. 'And then I'll wind up in the Solomon Islands!' —
'I expect so!' he said. 'Iconoclast of the Islands! A Conrad
    in reverse! Lord Ken!' —
He said: 'David's doing damn fine out there, —
Bigman Chief of Fuckwire Island and all that —
But time now draweth nigh for the Great Smasher of Icons —
    (those frozen moments of myth!) —
And I speak here of the ethics of cannibalism! —
Why do you think we sent back the soul of Richard Burton

to infest Anthony Hopkins? —
In order to give the guy the charisma to play Hannibal Lecter! —
And now you've had Jeffrey Dahmer! —
and some splendid tart's been at it! —
EATING PEOPLE IS BACK! —
Bone up on your Dodd! —
We'll tell you when we're ready for you in the cradle of
    cannibalism —
David's already conquered the Northern islands, you'll move
    in at the South —
You'll meet up round about Fukkabukka —' —
I said: 'What and then I'll have to eat David?' —
'See how it goes!' he said, and he came forward, and he
    gripped me lovingly by the upper arm:
'There'll be pies,' he said —
'Excuse me —
There is something I must do —' —
And the whole theophany —
(or Captophany as it turned out to be) —
had lasted a mere nanosecond . . .

The Solomon Islanders embraced Christianity under the impression that they would thereby receive the wealth and possessions of the White Man. When this did not happen for them, they supposed they'd been tricked. That they'd been given cut or censored Bibles with the magic missing. It's now reliably reported that on the islands of Malakula, Erromango, and Tafea, that the gags and routines of Kenneth Dodd* are regarded as the lost gospels. And if on the 13th of March I'm called to join that priesthood 'tis with a sense of honour I shall chomp upon the Host.

*That's where I whisk off the wartyfala mask revealing the Melanesian Devotional Doddy, sometimes to an audible gasp.

Jamais Vu

A slight, white-bearded man wearing nothing but a fringed straw penis guard, Chief Jack shows them his signed photograph of Prince Philip, his Coronation biscuit tin and – even more bizarrely – a glossy magazine featuring Ken Dodd.

This was donated by a visiting British actor who sends the chief postcards signed Prettyboy Tentringer, explaining in pidgin that Ken Dodd is 'man blong laf blong Prince Philip'.

Lindsey Hilsum
Guardian, 20 August 1993

Written and performed by Ken Campbell, *Jamais Vu* was premièred at the Cottesloe, Royal National Theatre, London, on 7 October 1993 and subsequently transferred to the Vaudeville Theatre, London

Music by Richard Kilgour
Artwork by Mitch Davies
Paintings by Derek Cowie and Gavin Gibson
Research by James Nye

Directed by Colin Watkeys

The National Theatre is a military fortress, temporarily housing
   the Arts —
Its formidable windowless design, its only openings towards
   the river —
is a giveaway as to its primary purpose:
to defend a certain élite in time of extreme urban disturbance.
There is an identical building on Merseyside —
(in this case, it temporarily houses insurance) —
and several more are planned.
In every National Theatre audience
(disguised as regular punters) —
are National Fortress officials,
with hidden agenda should things erupt outside.
Underneath are cavernous vaults —
and an array of arms, gas, and water cannon.
The vaults are linked with the whole secret tunnel system
   of the Capital.

I got this possibly classified information from a retired barrister,

who I was treating to a cup of tea outside the National Film
Theatre —
The barrister's practice and marriage had fallen apart —
due to bad breath —
and he now preferred to live with his dog – in a box.
'Your breath seems all right now,' I said —
'Ohhh! this life suits me better,' he said —
'I think the breath was a cry for help —
There's gotta be some place for us savages.'
He referred to judges as 'law students who get to mark their
    own papers'.
'Does it ever shake you,' he said,
'that there's only one Monopolies Commission?' —

We wandered the few yards over to the Open Book Market —
The barrister showed me the extraordinary bits in Whitaker's
    book *Diana v. Charles* about the bugging of the Royals —
Who might be doing it —
How —
Conversations are picked up from floor and window vibrations
    from miles away —
and it prints the whole Camillagate tape:

> *Charles*: Oh God, I'll just live inside your trousers or some-
> thing. It would be much easier!
> *Camilla (laughs)*: What are you going to turn into? A pair of
> knickers? (*Both laugh.*) Oh, you're going to come back as
> a pair of knickers.
> *Charles*: Oh, God forbid, a Tampax, just my luck! (*Laughs.*)
> *Camilla*: You are a complete idiot! (*Laughs.*) Oh, what a
> wonderful idea.
> *Charles*: My luck to be chucked down the lavatory and go
> on and on forever swirling round the top, never going down!

Camilla (laughing): Oh, darling!*

(Did you know that as a child Di was obsessed by the Weather
    Forecast? —
at the age of five she was known for her Weather Forecast
    impressions!) —
Referring to what we're up to with our Royals:

PHILIP'S KICK IN THE GOULASH
He calls the Hungarians a load of old potbellies
                                                    – Daily Star

SUD ORF!
Queen stops free soap for servants in perks shake up at
the Palace
                                                    – The Sun

the barrister said:
'Isn't it a bit like you've got an old dog —
and you're undecided as to whether to have the thing put down —
so to help you make up your mind . . .
you torture it.'

I'd been summoned to the National Theatre by a phone call
    from Richard Eyre's office —
'Are you planning on doing any more of those one-man
    shows?' —
'Yes,' I said.
(Actually, I hadn't really —
I'd squeezed my life dry of material already with the other two) —
'So that'd make three, wouldn't it?' —
'Mm' —
'So, it'd be a trilogy?' —

*James Whitaker, *Diana v. Charles*, Signet 1993.

'Mn' yes' —
'Well, it's possible you could open your new one here,
if you're prepared to do all three on one of the days' —
Blimey! —
'It's the year of the trilogy, you see' —
'Oh,' I said, 'I didn't know that. Is that generally? Or just
    at your place?' —
'Well no. We're doing three David Hare plays all on one
    day, you see —
and we're calling that a trilogy —
and so if we had yours on, it would seem like trilogies are
    in the wind.'

So I'd set off with my case and zimmer combination —
there wasn't much in it —
but it gets you through the beggars —
Outside Waterloo station I'd popped round to that hardware
    store and bought several sink plungers —
enough I hoped to get me through this preliminary meeting.
I saw that John Birt was to be on stage at the National Film
    Theatre that night,
talking live to Jeremy Isaacs (who was also going to be live) —
I took my leave of the boxed barrister and nipped in and
    bought a ticket for that,
and then hastened off to the National Fortress —
'*Royal* National Theatre' —

'You know about the Hare Trilogy?' (Richard Eyre) —
'Yes,' I said. 'I understand you want a Bald Trilogy?' —
'Exactly! Very good. We can use that —

Now, what will the third one be about?'
I'd no idea —
To hold him off I said:
'You know about Artist's Choice?' —
'Tell us' —
Well basically there are held to be three choices:
One: (which is possible) —
You can distract, entertain, *and deceive about the true state
    of things* —
and thus help to sustain the status quo —
(including its wrongs) —
or —
Two: (which is also possible) —
You can *pose* as exposing the wrongs, but in fact deceive —
and therefore still be helping to sustain them.
Either of these can lead to OBEs and knighthoods —
and —
Three: (which alas is not possible) —
You can expose wrongs and bring about change —
Not possible, because if you know what's really going on you
    have to sign a thing saying you won't tell anyone, not even,
    (in fact *especially* not) the Prime Minister.
But I'm suggesting there might be a *Fourth* – which might
    be possible:
To *pose* as exposing wrongs,
but in fact *deceive* but with a wilful mix of truth and lie, research
    and fantasy, so inscrutably compounded as to send the status
    quo hunting for needles that nobody's lost, in haystacks that
    don't exist, diverting attention from the ensuing release of
    hitherto imprisoned forces, which *will* bring about change,
    but of an unpredictable nature.'
'We take it you'll be going for the fourth?' —
'Yes. Maybe not stand-up comedy —
SIT-DOWN TRAGEDY! —
a comic epic science-fiction conspiracy-weepie!' —
'You are aware,' said Richard, 'that our audiences aren't as

bright as the ones you're used to?' —
'No . . .' —
'You're used to your own loyal little bunch who turn up in
   some part-converted bacon-curing works, and they've really
   come to *be* there —
a lot of ours just come to *have been* there' —
'Oh. So I should make it short?' —
'Oh no! Ours like to suffer – that's all become part of it.
   They expect that.
I'm just a bit worried —
You see, our last one-man show was this dangling French-
   Canadian . . .
Our audience might be a bit phased if they find themselves
   following yours' —
'Oh. So – make it obscure?' —
'Oh yes, make it obscure, but not so obscure it couldn't be
   cleared up in a few lines by Billington —
Have you any ideas how you'll structure this one? —
You used a hatstand, didn't you, for *Pigspurt*, your last one?' —
'That's right,' I said. 'Six contrasting narrative strands held
   by a centrepiece common to them all' —
'And the centrepiece is God, isn't it,' said Richard —
'coming through the wall at the end?'
'Yes' —
'And for this one?' —
'Well, I was thinking of basing it on a sink plunger,' I said —
'Act One will be circular —
In Act Two, we will realize that we had in fact been experiencing
   the base of a dome —
Act Three: the handle' —
'Phallic!' said Richard —
'And also volcanic – like an upsurge of lava! —
Will you have a plunger on stage with you?' —
'Yes' —
'And you'll justify its presence?' —
'Yes' —

'How will you do that?'

And I found myself telling him about Eddie Davis —
my late mate —
By the time I knew him, Ed was an old man —
Some men, when they get old, look like babies —
And Ed was one of those: —
a tubby, chubby, old baby —
quite simply, you fell in love with him, and wanted to play
    with him —
Totally bald —
always wore a hat: just slightly small —
He gave his profession as: 'Eccentric Dancer, and Hokum
    Maniac' —
Ed wasn't the sort of artiste to whom the likes of Eyre could
    have said:
'Now, now, Edward, I think the author only intended titters
    here . . .' —
Ed was a hunter of the WILD GUFFAW —
and once he had one of them in his sights —
he needed HYSTERIA —
an audience HELPLESS —
BEGGING FOR *LESS*! —
Like a lot of those old timers (Max Wall, the Crazy Gang, etc.)
Ed had the knack of suddenly so excruciating his body,
that some audience members (particularly the older ones) would
    literally *pee* themselves —
In the thirties Ed had toured in the comedy-thriller *Poison
    Piano* —
He played Toes Petersen, the deaf-mute armless amputee who
    plays the piano with his feet —
And in the Third Act climax when Toes learns that:
the poison is in the trousers! —

Ed's portrayal of the hapless, armless Toes, trying to divest
   his wobbly legs of the plague-soiled pants —
Up the walls! —
On the piano! —
And in Cardiff he'd hit it! —
He'd hit the Hokum High! —
Clanged the Lost Chord of Comedy! —
and the Cardiff audience was laughing —
weeping —
groaning —
shrieking —
choking —
farting —
poohing —
weeing —
folding —
and some Welshmen actually **EXPLODING** and **EXPIRING** in
   their own juices and wastes —
'How did you do that?' I asked —
'I wouldn't tell you if I knew . . .' he said —
'You don't realize the awesome power of comedy —
it can kill' —
'How do you feel about it now? Any regrets?' —
Ed thought —
and then he said:
'I just comfort myself that it was Welshmen.'

His last job was in a tour of *My Fair Lady* —
He had three lines as one of Dolittle's men —
Peter Bayliss as Dolittle at one point had to thump Ed on
   the head —
One night there'd been a sink block in the dressing room —
and Ed suggested to Bayliss that instead of thumping him,

he rammed the sink plunger on his head —
It was a hit!
Ed was then in and out of hardware stores —
amassing plungers, timing their different performances —
assessing suction coefficients —
and it was such a yell, he had to have his own personal curtain call.
Then it was the last date before London —
and Gillian Lynn, the choreographer, was adamant:
Eddie had to go —
On Saturday, she said: 'He took the curtain call with six plungers
    on his head! —
My Fair Lady just isn't about sink plungers —
. . . and there've been more complaints of wet seats' —
But Peter Bayliss said: 'If Eddie goes, I go —
He listens to me. Let him stay' —
So Eddie stayed, and they cut the sink plunger for the previews
    and press night,
and every subsequent performance that Gillian Lynn was in for —
But the producers *loved* it —
'We've got important people in – Eddie *will* be doing his
    plunger? —
Gillian's in Leeds . . .' —
'Yeah' —

'And you'll actually put a plunger on your head in your show?'
    said Richard —
'Yes, I'll have it on quite near the beginning. Maybe as a
    set up for the end, and I'll put it on again for the climax —
'cause – in case there's any need for heavy philosophizing
    at the end —
it'll lighten it' —
'Good, yes,' said Richard. 'And it'll be something for all those
    who aren't following it to look at —
that was the genius of LePage's dangling interludes —

Can you get six on?' —

'You do realize,' said Richard, 'that we're not going to just
    let you go on —
We've got to know that you've got something to tell us —
You're off to Australia aren't you?' —
'Yes,' I said —
'When?' he said —
'In a couple of weeks,' I said —
'Where?' —
'Sydney' —
'How about if you go to Vanuatu while you're in.that part?' —
'Hmn?' —
'The Republic of Vanuatu is those South Pacific Islands that
    used to be the New Hebrides' —
He handed me a guidebook* of the area —
'Since they went independent in 1980, loads of them have
    reverted from Christianity —
Cargo Cults – and all that sort of thing —
and volcanoes,' said Richard stroking a plunger —
'Go to Vanuatu and come back with some sort of comedy
    anthropology maybe? —
Anyway, try and give us a positive proposal, before you go
    to Australia.'
'I think that might be where they worship Ken Dodd,' I said.

It was the week that John Birt's alleged ploy of having his com-
    pany employed by the BBC rather than himself, and paying his

---

*David Harcombe, *Vanuatu – a travel survival kit*, Lonely Planet Publications, Australia, 1991.

missus thirty grand a year for not doing ever so much really —
had pushed the Royal Family off the front page —
and the NFT auditorium was packed with folk gathered for
   the sport of watching the great squirm.

First thing I note is this:
You see, to have full, sexy, kissable lips like mine, you have
   to have gone Bllmbllmbllm a lot as a child —
it was clear that the infant Birt hadn't had the wit to do this —
He is *virtually lipless* —

Jeremy Isaacs played Birt like a great angler —
But it was as if there were no fish —
It was extraordinary how little charisma Birt had —
an almost negative presence —
You can't hold on to what John Birt has just said —
while he's saying it, it seems clear enough —
But then *it's like trying to grab hold of a lump of raw liver
   while sitting in a bath of engine oil* —
'The Man Who Fell to Earth —
An *alien*, inadequately briefed,' I wrote in my notebook —

Maybe the problem was this:
BBC personnel objected to being laid off by *him* —
A big jolly man, or a gorilla – a Maxwell! 'Fair cop guv
   – game's up' —
and they'd've buggered off —

but to be dismissed by someone whose prime gift seemed to
  be that of retrospective absence . . .

at the end of the do, you remember little more than the
  glasses and the Armani suit.

I had a motive for being in that audience —
I was an addict, and John Birt was one of the big dealers.
I was an addict of TV news.
To be sure, sometimes I could get past breakfast without a fix —
sometimes lunchtime —
but at twenty to six, six o'clock, Channel Four at seven o'clock —
nine o'clock, ten o'clock —
and grab a quick beer to settle in with *Newsnight* —
But the more I watched —
the less I knew —
It was as if it were sucking knowledge from me —
draining me of things I had known *before* —
My mind must have been somewhere while I was watching it —
But where? —
I could never retrieve it —
And the awful void into which my addiction was plunging
  me was having effect on other areas of my life —
For example, I was sitting on the toilet and noticed we'd
  run out of paper —
And there was no one in —
so I'd hobbled downstairs to get the kitchen roll —
to find I'd returned with a spoon —
Where had my mind been? —
And I'd lost possession of my own face —

I'd forgotten what the silly thing is meant to look like when
   you're taking an intelligent interest in what someone's saying
   to you —
and while I'm worrying about that —
I don't know what they're saying —

Shamble off home.
And Paxman.
And Paxman's enviable knowledge of his own face —
He really *inhabits* his face —
Will that simple ability ever be mine again? —

I felt the need to stretch out and see if there are any fellow
   sufferers out there —
I decided to interview the public at large —
Get the man-in-the-street's views of television – content and
   technology of —
To do this, I adopted a disguise:
Wig —
facsimile Mellor Dentures – David Mellor teeth —
(I like my Mellors —
they give you the look of possibly going to be witty in a minute) —

Cream of the results:

'My eldest daughter is zombified, and I'm sure it's the telly —
because if I try and switch it off she bites me.'

'TV is an alien which is eating my brain —
but it keeps not being the day to do anything about it.'

'My sister threw her television out, and she's never looked
    so well —
I wish I had the courage to do that.'

A woman whose son gets sent into fits by the telly —
whatever the programme.

And here's a woman whose husband had a dream: —
'and the television wasn't on, but he dreamed of three winners:
horses —
but the way he'd dreamed it, he was watching the telly —
the horse racing —
and when he woke up, he'd found he'd got it right: absolutely
    right —

but it wasn't just that he'd dreamed winners —
that was what was on the telly —
So he'd received the broadcast directly into his brain —
and he'd got nothing peculiar about him —
a few fillings in his teeth —
nothing else.'

A man in Birmingham who's got a tin plate in his head (for
  some reason) —
and he's permanently tuned to Channel Four —
and he got them to take that plate out and put in another one —
and now he still gets Channel Four —
but *blurry* —
and he prefers to have it clear if he's got to have it —
so he's asking them to put the old one back.

Then there was that week . . .
I was nearly run over twice in one week by the same car —
or was the second occasion a case of déjà vu? . . .
And then —
Did either event actually happen?
And that's when we're slipping on the dangerous ice of *jamais vu.*

Déjà vu is when you go somewhere and you've never been
  there before,
and you get the feeling: *I've been here before —*
Jamais vu —
is when you go home and you say:
'*Fuck, I've never been here before!*' —
The wife comes in and you think, 'Who's that?' —

Did you ever go back to see a film again —
but your favourite moment *isn't in it*? —
And you re-read a book, and they've changed the plot —
And there was this guy in the Almost Free Hospital in
   Hampstead —
a patient —
and he woke up to find an alien in his bed —
and it was growing out of one of his buttocks —
anyway, he was punching it and wrestling it, and wound up
   on the floor with it —
and he was trying to strangle it, when he noticed the frightful
   thing didn't have hair exactly . . .
It had TOES! —
He'd had JAMAIS VU of his own LEG! —

We'd been promised that John Birt would take questions from
   the floor —
and I was preparing a query on these phenomena —
when suddenly, John Birt wasn't there —
A man at the back shouted:
'Hoy, Mr Birt – I thought there were gonna be questions!' —
But he was gone.

Anyway, I was having a pee next to the guy who'd shouted out —
He knew who I was (he'd seen *Pigspurt*) —
And we had a cup of tea in the NFT café —
'Did you actually see John Birt go?' (his name was Oliver) —
'No, not really – I suddenly realized he'd gone' —
'Birt is amazing,' said Oliver —
'He's surrounded —

the Birt knockers are all round him —
they're firing off their salvoes —
BUT THEY CAN'T HIT HIM! —
they just maim each other! —
That Jeremy Isaacs is sharp —
he was firing live rounds, wasn't he? —
But did he hit him? —
ONCE!? —
John Birt is a Master of Negative Hallucination,' said Oliver —
(A Master of Positive Hallucination – like Mesmer —
can make you see things that aren't there —
a Master of Negative Hallucination —
like Gurdjieff, Crowley and MacGregor Mathers —
can make you *not* see things that *are* there) —
'Birt was diverting attention from himself and then
    PARALYSING TIME! —
He invokes a cloud of *NOT TO BE ENQUIREDINTONESS* —
He only allows your Unconscious to perceive him —
and then he inhibits the Unconscious from any traffic with
    the Conscious —
so you recall him no more than a dream' —
(Hearing all this, I was in fact becoming a fan of John Birt —
I couldn't wait not to see him again) —
Anyway, 'What was the question you were going to ask?'
    I asked Oliver —
And this is it: (wow!) —
'Jesus, Napoleon and the Emperor of the South Pacific are still
    the favourites for deluded schizophrenics to suppose they are,
    but coming in now at number seventeen, is John Birt. Does
    Mr Birt have any intention of visiting these unfortunates? If
    so, would he welcome a list of the establishments where they
    may be found?' —
I said, 'Really? What – there are people who think they're
    John Birt?' —
'Oh yes,' he said —
I said, 'What – and you've met them?' —

'I've met *some*. Yes,' he said —
'How come?' —
'Oh, I'm into computers and everything,' he said —
(?) —
'What are they like?' —
'Silly mostly, but there's one in the Uxbridge Regional Secure
    Unit who I think would amuse you' —
'Can you get me in to see him?' —
'Sure' —
A couple of days later I was walking the dog in Finsbury Park —
A shout from behind:
'Oy Ken!' —
A guy in a wheelchair speeding towards me like he was in
    a wheelchair marathon —
He had a potty hat on —
'Ken!' —
I didn't think I knew him —
and I didn't —
he'd recognized me from a photo of me on the back of my
    *Old King Cole** script —
and he'd been in it! —
he'd played the Baron apparently, in an all-wheelchair
    production.
I said, 'How terrific! But usually when people recognize me,
    it's from some crap on the box' —
He said (and this is the interesting bit) *he hadn't watched
    TV for years* —
TV – videos even – gave him fits —
TV had fucked his oculo-endocrine system —
I said, 'Is that why you're in a wheelchair?' —
He said no —
that's *why* he'd watched so much TV his oculo-endocrine system
    was fucked —
And now he was a stand-up comedian —

*Ken Campbell, *Old King Cole*, Oberon Books Ltd, 32 Russell Road, Enfield, Middlesex EN1
4TY. Tel: 0181-367-9603.

(except for the standing-up bit) —
and he wanted to talk about comedy —
and Jake (his name) asked me if I'd seen Billy Connolly at
    Hammersmith —
I had —
'What d'you think?' —
I said, 'Great – but he doesn't half say Fuck a lot!' —
'He does say Fuck a lot, doesn't he? – three or four times
    a sentence —
He even splits up words now to shove a Fuck up them:
"They're tarmacfuckingadaming the roads" —
He never used to do that, did he?'
'No' —
'Now, I've been a follower – a devotee of Connolly,' says Jake —
'and maybe he'd have said Fuck three times in an evening —
but this is something else! —
My night, he split up a Fuck to shove a Fuck up it —
"FUCKFUCKING HELLING HELL" he said —
Well I gotta look into where the master's leading us —
it doesn't start till he starts nobbing with the Royal Family —
and that's how they go on – they're EFFING and blinding
    way beyond troupers —
all of them (apparently) —
and Connolly was *freaked* —
he reckoned something sinister was going on,
and he couldn't put his finger on it —
So his act at Hammersmith was like saying:
"Notice somebody, won't you? The incredible difference in
    my act: —
I've shaved, look, and I'm saying Fuck nineteen times a minute —
and where have I just been? – who have I just been with? —
Pick up! somebody —
Ask! somebody" —
and he was under the impression that something appalling had
    happened to the Royal Family —
he couldn't do more —

and then he kept nearly getting run over by the same car,
and he scrammed off to be a Yank sitcom tart —
Is it here now? Have you seen it?' —
I said, No – I only watched news —
and I didn't watch that now.

Jake was on his way back from his sister's funeral —
'Same problem,' he said, chirpily tapping his wheelchair —
(He was Mr Chirpy) —
I said, 'How do you keep so cheerful? You must have a
    secret . . .' —
He said, 'Well, they never really go from us, do they?' —
I said, 'No . . .' —
He said, 'Come on Ken, you must have a lot of dead people
    in your life by now' —
I said, 'Yeah, well I've got a few, thanks' —
And he said, 'And don't they sometimes come into your mind,
    focused and clear?' —
I said, 'Yeah' —
'Well,' he said, 'then you should say "hello" —
"Hi Dad!" "Hi Doris!" – whatever' —
He said, if he was ever blue, he used a dicknose and laughing
    mirror —
and he gave me his set —
'There are more in stock in St Albans,' he told me —
(Actually . . . it works) —
I said, 'You might be just the chap I need —
I'm going to be doing a show at the National Theatre and
    I'm looking for ideas' —
'I'll give you an act'll go down a bomb there,' he said —
'The Great Spunko' —
Apparently you get announced as the Great Spunko —
and you just come out and stand in front of the audience

with your hands in your pockets —
but what they don't realize is one of your arms is a false arm —
and you just stand there for a bit —
and then your secret real arm (which is down the inside of
  your shirt) undoes your fly buttons from the inside and then
  lets off shaving foam —
He said it wasn't a long act – more an attention-getter.
I said, 'Have you ever been to the National Theatre?' —
He said he hadn't —
I said, No, it was a great act – but he should keep it —
No, he said – he'd tried it, but it was tasteless from a wheel-
  chair.
I said, 'No – it's the Royal National Theatre —
It's not actually *acts* I'm looking for —
more a central issue —
a great goal: a quest' —
He hadn't realized it was the ROYAL National Theatre —
He said, 'Well, why don't you carry on with Connolly's work?' —
I said, 'What do you mean?' —
He said: 'Well, save the Queen . . . save the monarchy' —
I said, 'Really?' —
He said, 'Well, if Connolly thought it was worthwhile, I'm
  sure it is.'

Can you see the attraction of this notion? —
. . . if I began my show with the barrister and his bad breath —
and the Queen & Co. being some old dog we're torturing —
I dunno, and then some other stuff —
and then this meeting with Jake and his extraordinary insight
    into Billy Connolly's relationship with the Royal Family —
that would in some sense be sort of circular . . .

I'd be Act One done —
and onto 'the dome'.

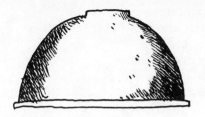

But:
Save the Queen . . .?
Save the monarchy . . .?
Why? . . .
And precisely what from? —

The Uxbridge Regional Secure Unit is round the back of
    what in the 1800s, when the asylum was built, had been a
    brewery —
The lunatics brewed beer as a business,
and it was loaded onto barges at the Grand Union Canal
    at the back —
But now they're turning it into an alcoholics' detox unit —
(circular!) —
Double doors – a turnstile – and a man in an office: —
We turn out our pockets – (me and Oliver) —
Man in office takes my keys and matches —
takes Oliver's Swiss Army knife —
'Nothing else? —
'No . . . Afro combs?' —
'No' —
and Oliver and me are led by a dangerously thin Irish orderly
    up a corridor and into a dining room —
Round tables and chairs —

dirty cups everywhere —
patients on settees in the TV corner.
We crunch to a table —
loads of cornflakes on the floor.
Henry Katz is the name of the man Oliver's brought me to see —
'I don't know where he is,' says ludicrously thin Irishman —
'He refuses all OT,' (Occupational Therapy) 'so he should
    be around —
ahh, here he is' —
Katz had overheard.
'They lay on gardening, gym, art, psychotherapy, drama therapy,
    discussion groups once a week, massage, keep fit, pottery and
    sports —
But I refuse it all,' said Henry Katz genially —
'I prefer to sit around and smoke, and eat cornflakes —
It annoys the staff – which is pleasing in itself —
but it also means they can't wait to get rid of you —
We get through a lot of cornflakes but we have difficulty
    getting it into the bowls —
It's the medication.'
I could see a garden with a bird table —
a lady with fat legs was feeding ducks —
Katz looked past Oliver and directly at me —
'You stopped having clearly focused erotic dreams about the
    Queen in 1979,' he said —
'If you say so,' I said —
'I do say so, because that's when those particular psychotronical
    broadcasts stopped' —
Henry Katz looked faintly familiar —
. . . somewhere, I'd seen him before —
Katz wore glasses like John Birt's —
He had a small box on his head – not much bigger than
    a matchbox —
a bit like a miniature tape recorder —
He explained that his corpus callosum had been split —
(the brain is in two halves linked by the corpus
    callosum) —

and the severed ends of his two brain halves had been
  reconnected through the box,
which monitored and modified the thought traffic as it passed
  between one brain hemisphere and the other —
inside the box, was the mind of John Birt, who'd had a similar
  operation performed, but in his case in order to download his
  mind into a computer —
so he could have back-up copies of himself —
'I'm one of the experiments to see if he can't have user-friendly
  wetware,' Katz explained —
I said, 'But I saw John Birt the other day at the NFT
  thing with Jeremy Isaacs, and he hadn't got any box on his
  head' —
Katz said, 'It's all built into his glasses – he's got a plug-in
  stud on the frames' —
I said, 'And you say there are others who are becoming
  John Birt downloaded wetware?' —
'Oh, I know another two. Sometimes we all meet together' —
'Where?' —
Well, sometimes here – or Broadmoor, or the Reading RSU' —
'Who are the others?' —
'A couple of old luvvies' —
'And have the luvvies all got boxes on their heads?' —
'Yes' —
Then Katz said, 'And sometimes John comes to our dos . . .
But not necessarily encumbered with his body' —
(I could see this was not going to be a wasted afternoon . . .)
I said, 'How does he pay for all this? – they've put him
  on PAYE now' —
'Oh, they'll give him a rise, won't they,' Katz said, 'to cover
  that shortfall —
but anyway he doesn't pay for *this*' (his box) —
'Who does?' —
Katz looked at Oliver who nodded that it was safe to continue —
'The IAE,' said Katz. 'The Ice Age Élite' —
I looked blank —
(Well, I don't know whether I looked blank,
  but I *felt* blank –) —

Where did I know this guy from?
We'd met – I knew his voice from somewhere —
And then I saw his cycle clips —
Did you notice the cycle clips, Watson?
What of them, Holmes?
Where would he go biking off to locked up in a secure unit . . . ?
I said: 'Did you used to use the Gants Hill Library?' —
'Yes,' he said —
Suddenly I felt at home.

I left the Royal Academy of Dramatic Art in 1960 as a
    fully trained comic actor —
But Ned Sherrin and people like that had the power —
The David Frost/Monty Python successes meant they were
    only looking for comedians with a university education —
It wasn't enough to be amusing and have read the newspapers —
you had to have read newspapers at Cambridge —
Not being a lot in demand meant being back home with my dad —
And I went down to the Gants Hill Library to give myself
    an education —
And I found the Basement —
and I joined the camaraderie of the Basement —
In the Basement you could make a noise —
In the Basement were the Books That No One Had Ever
    Taken Out —
Many never opened —
The Gants Hill Library Basement was some sort of depot for
    all the books in the area that no one was reading – or there'd
    been complaints about —
I had the idea that if I read all the books that no one else was
    reading, it would make me special —
It would distinguish me —
and my ascendancy above the Herd would be assured —
I was in error:

it would *estrange* me from the Herd —
In your formative years you must have a directed reading list —
No matter that in some basement you will exhume something
   more vital, more alarming than the official syllabus —
You will be unwelcome in the Herd's clubs.
Sometimes people say I'm mad —
I'm not mad! Arsehole! —
I've just read different books!
And Katz was one of the Guys from the Basement, the
   Gants Hill Basement —
Katz used to have a very black friend, and they used to
   plough through missionary books together —
And he always wore a beret and cycle clips —
but he didn't have a bike —
It was his library style —
And it was Katz who'd asked me one time if that librarian
   girl was bothering me —
I said, 'No, she's quite sweet really' —
He'd said, 'Well, if you want to get rid of her, put a bit
   of cotton wool in your ear —
it keeps women at bay —
the idea sinks in subliminally that maybe you're a bit waxy,
and they leave you alone' —
And it's a good tip —
(My cousin [this was last year] got these awful ear growths
   from his mobile phone —
and he had to wad his ear out —
and his marriage [agreed already shaky] didn't last the week!) —

Down in the basement we could kick up a din —
and we used to arge and barge and debate the days away —
But something united us —
Put into words it'd go something like:

*Don't **believe** in anything* —
Nothing which is the product of the human mind is a fitting
   subject for belief —
'Religion' comes from the root *religare* – 'to bind' —
Religion is *the lies that bind you* —
But you can suppose *everything*: —
and in fact you should —
Supposing as much as poss is mind-opening, mind-widening —
Suppose God —
suppose flying saucers —
suppose fairies —
I suppose you could suppose that one of the Big Religions
   had got it right —
to the last nut and bolt! —
But don't *believe* it! —
If you really believe your belief is IT, it would be what
   the Greeks called 'hubris' —
and it would be very nasty for you and all concerned —
(and possibly some innocent bystanders too) —
It was Katz who wrote the Gants Hill Hymn:

> *Onward Christian soldiers, onward Buddhist priests,*
> *Onward fruits of Islam, fight till you're deceased!*
> *Fight in richest battle, fight to trumpet shrill!*
> *For the greater glory, o-o-of Gants Hill!*
> *Rah-rah rah-rah rah-rah rah-rah – phthhhbpt!*

Foolishly, I sang it to my dad —
and my dad got a bit alarmed about the company I
   was keeping at the Gants Hill Library —

He was great my dad – he always did things in a humorous way —
(In the war he'd been a wireless Morse telegraphist —
he taught me Morse at a very young age —

Did you know this?:
The Morse for a laugh is MIM —
— — ● ● — —
two dashes two dots two dashes —
Because that's what it sounds like: HaHa HeHe HaHa!) —

Anyway, Dad'd just won a consolation prize in a slogan
   competition —
Lever's Soap wanted a new jingle for their shaving soap —
and my dad had sent in:

What shaved the face of dirty Dick? —
Why Lever's Easy-Shaving Stick!

and won a hundred sticks of the stuff —
'Here,' he said, handing me a dozen —
'some of your friends at the library *might want to take up*
   shaving' —
And I'd given Katz one —
and he'd looked at it, and then looked to his black friend —
and then he tossed it – *bong!* – in the waste paper can —
'The last war,' he said, 'was fought between the baddies who
   turned Jews into soap to wash their awful German bodies,
   and the goodies who turned the South Pacific Islanders into
   soap to wash their fine British bodies' —
I never forgot that —
I'd no idea what he'd meant —
But it's a stopper at parties.
But with the excitement of Katz's next revelations, I neglected
   the opportunity to ask him —
I said, 'How did you get into this line, Henry?' (pointing
   at his box) —
'You get recruited through the TV,' he said —
'Both the technology and programme content of TV are

behaviour modifiers —
Television and cinema are fundamentally different —
in the cinema, the pictures are projected onto a screen,
and you look at them on the screen —
with TV, a Cathar Ray fires directly into your brain through
    pixels and whatnot —
and the image is *assembled in your head* —
and Cathar Rays are *dangerous* —
for example they stuck a load of sparrows in front of a
    TV and just transmitted green at them —
result? – the female sparrows went infertile —
and the male sparrows' bollocks grew so big they couldn't fly –' —
'TV fucks your oculo-endocrine system, doesn't it,' I said —
'Burns it out,' said Katz —
I said, 'What actually is your oculo-endocrine system?' —
He said, 'Well, your eyes is just your brain peeping out
    from time to time, isn't it?' —
I said, 'So you get recruited subliminally through the TV?' —
To this he replied: 'Well let's say you get *softened* by the TV —
Then if they pick up that you're *potential* . . .' —
'How do *they* do that?' —
'Well one way is with the Licence Detector Vans —
then they modify your behaviour directly – psychotronically —
they fire programmes through your telly —
individually tailored to your requirements —
or rather, their requirements of you —
your TV and radio start to address you directly —
(a lot go completely up the pictures at that point) —
but if you handle that, then they move on to Phase Two:
direct broadcasting (or narrowcasting) into the brain and
    nervous system —
intercranial channelling —
psychotronical broadcasting from Licence Detector Vans and
    also satellites' —
'What happens then?!' —
'You start to act weird —

find yourself answering ads you'd never normally answer —
doing nutty things that add up to nothing —
contradictory self-cancelling actions —
mumbling occult mumbo jumbo behind Jewish ladies in
    Safeways —
and suddenly your internal systems ROAR —
and you just get on with IT —
you'll supply reasons later – if there's a LATER! —
You're running round like a damaged rat —
you can't get off the Circle Line —
there's a bomb at every station —
and you're the bomb —
and you wind up some place like this —
and eventually they make you an offer —
You know those things they use for bugging the Royals from
    six miles away and more? —
Well, the same technology with little modification can *fire* —
But of course the Royals have been psychotronicked for a
    punishing time —
Charles, Di and Fergie are little more than damaged rats now —
With the younger ones, it's just a question of firing in behaviour
    modifications —
mainly into the pleasure centres and sex drives' —
Interestingly, Katz had a soft spot for the Duchess of York —
He said:
'No vibrant young woman would put her foot into an accountant's
    mouth,
unless she'd been got at by psychotronical gizmos —
The Duke's tough, but they've *crusted* him —
I'm not being too technical?' —
'No' —
'Crusting:
He used to bark orders —
now he just barks;
barking out of windows —
A man of very powerful thought —

Of course, he was offered a place in the IAE —
but he turned it down' —
'What's this IAE . . . ? You say this IAE – the Ice Age
    Élite (?) offered the Duke of Edinburgh a place, and to pay
    for boxes for you and the luvvies?' —
'The Ice Age Élite . . .' said Katz —
'Global Warming: Hole in the Ozone Layer –
    ALL A FRONT! —
Disinformation —
The Rhythm of Things on Earth is this:
a million years of Ice Age – or "glacial" —
and then ten thousand years of this – what we're enjoying
    the last few minutes of now:
INTER-GLACIAL —
We were due for our next Ice Age just after Shagspur —
but the fumes from the industrial revolution fucked it' —
'So we'll be alright as long as we keep the fumes going? —
maintain the pollution levels?' —
BUT NO —
Apparently there's been a mutation in the algal plankton
    of the oceans —
mutated algal plankton is taking in the CO_2 and the CFCs
    and everything —
and breeding like a fury, and giving off clouds of dimethyl
    sulphide —
which is significantly reflecting back the sun's rays, cooling
    the Earth —
which is opening and cracking the volcanic faults, Philippines
    and everywhere —
volcanic dust clouds responsible for further cooling —
AND THE ICE CAPS ARE NOW ADVANCING —
the increase in snow and ice adding an albedo (like albino)
    effect —
'And an Ice Age takes only twenty years to regain its WHITE
    GLORY —
(We're talking about London under
    a mile of snow here!) —

and the Ice Age Élite plan to sit it out in the warmish
    belts round the equator —
You can't halt an Ice Age, but you can hurry one on —
If the IAE are ready ahead of time,
they'll incinerate all America's garbage in remote parts of
    Canada —
the smoke blocks out the sun, and Our Lady of the Ice
    will be unstoppable —
Parts of Africa are to be used —
The French IAE are busy organizing a big plastic pipe to
    squirt the contents of the Rhône into Algeria —
and the Amazon River's 17 billion gallons an hour is gonna blast
    across the South Atlantic courtesy of 150-foot-diameter heavy
    plastic piping held to the sea bottom by cement ballast' —
He said, 'Why do you think there's this rage to recycle plastic? —
It used to be a menace – Now we need all we can get! —
And the islands of the South Pacific —
the French Ice Age Élite have been terrific there! —
They held onto Polynesia and the Marquesa Islands,
the Islands of New Caledonia – Nouvelle Caledonie – are
    still theirs —
and still *wan big influence* in the New Heb' —
'In what way terrific?' I asked —
'It's where they do their underground testing,' said Katz —
'and man! have they made headway!' —
'I thought underground nuclear testing was so you make less
    mess?' —
'Noooo!! Underground testing is to test what happens when
    you let these buggers off underground! —
Man! They've got the South Pacific mapped like a Chinese
    acupuncture chart —
so that when the smoke goes up from the Yank garbage
    they'll send their nukes down the hydrothermic vents of the
    ocean —
Through past the rocks and stuff of the Earth's crust —
and into the mantle where rock is hot bubbling liquid —

Tectonical engineering! —
This'll trigger off all the volcanic fault cores —
and they'll blast themselves up a whole new continent into
    being! —
They practise on Mururoa – but that's a front! —
The core detonation will come on Tanna – Yasur!' —

'They're into extremely advanced science then, the IAE?'
    I said —
'EXTREMELY advanced science,' said Katz —
'Man, they've cracked nanotechnology!' —
'Wow!' I said. Then: 'What is that?' —
'Assemblers for example – fleets of tiny atom-sized robots
    – self-replicating —
which can rework matter at the atomic level' —
'Doing what?' —
'Anything – well, let me qualify that —
For example, they've got a meat machine —
It does what a cow does, but without having to arse around
    with a cow —
You bung in a load of grass, and channel in some sunlight —
and you get a cabinet of meat —
That's what Chernobyl was all about —
They'd got a pork machine which went out of control —
It was bunging out pork at an exponential rate and it burst
    out of the cabinet —
And it'd've converted half the country into pork in a few hours —
so they blew it up —
And that's why the sheep on the Welsh hills were found
    ankle-deep in contaminated pork scratchings —
That is the danger with assemblers – it's called the Grey
    Goo Problem —
Oh! and they've reassembled a mouse —

I bring that up because I've seen it —
Birty brought one along to our last do at Broadmoor —
It's got no eyes, no teeth, no hair – like a deranged dong
    on the loose —
And here's the ringer – they don't scuttle away like regular
    mice —
they're programmed to make for you, and they hang onto
    you like limpets —
and you just pick 'em off yourself and pop 'em on the griddle —
they're as nutritious as rabbit – and it cuts out all that hunting
    bollocks —
And – you just have to scrape a few flakes off 'em —
and toss 'em in this soup (they call it soup, in fact it's a
    fertilizing agent) —
and wallop! —
half a hundred of the things!' —

I thought: Wow! – John Birt's come a long way since *Nice Time* —

'It's the trans-human condition, Kenneth!' he said, spilling
    cornflakes past the bowl —
'So now you see why it's vital to have John in there at the BBC —
to make sure programming continues to disgust the viewers
    with the world —
with themselves! —
News, documentaries, dramas, sitcoms, game shows, kiddy
    cartoons —
all must increase anxiety up the scale to *high anxiety* —
culminating in terror —
the Cathars' Ray opens you up, and John fires the business in —

which is our *kindness*,
so you welcome the final programme, when we up the BF —
Beat Frequency —
You know how opera singers can smash glasses with their
    voices? —
Well that's how Beat Frequency works —
Turns the brain and nervous system into junket and Jello —
And we can work it to a turn on all sets —
(maybe an ancient black and white set it'd only half work on) —
Certainly all Jap sets made in the last ten years —
And they're all fitted with "Presidential Over-rides" —
so they can be switched on by the transmitter even if they're
    not plugged in —
The BF waves will agitate the brain and nervous system
    pleasurably —
The ultimate vibrator! —
but reduce you to *silliness* —
too silly to do anything towards your own future —
amused to death —
Runcie saw the wisdom of it —
Because once the polar caps are really shifting,
the breakdown of civilization will be total!' —

QUAARCK!
Blood and gore hit the window —
The lady with the fat legs was seeing to a duck with an
    Afro comb - ! —
I said: 'Just say someone had to save the British monarchy
    in all this? —
How would they go about it?'
Katz thought —
'You'd have to start with the Duke —
He's strong —

and he's the only one of them who is a god – ' —
'Is he?' —
'Yes . . . he's worshipped
in Vanuatu — '

Vanuatu . . . Hmm . . .

'Why have you told me all this?' I said —
'Am I being recruited?' —
'You already were, Kenneth —
Some time ago . . .
Do you ever go back to the Gants Hill Library?' —
'I wouldn't know if it's still there,' I said —
'Go with the flow,' he said – 'Maybe those times will come
    back' —

It's great – when you meet again an old chum from way
    back when —
Especially when you find they haven't stood still —
He still had the old light —
His shaky hand wasn't age —
It was the medication.

IN THE MEN'S ROOM:
I said to Oliver:
'Is that true about upping the BF waves?' —
'No,' he said, 'it's crap – you'd have to lower the BF to do that' —
The spindly orderly came in for a slash —
'What's that thing on Mr Katz's head?' I asked him —
'It's a television remote,' said the orderly —
'Well – why's he got it on his head?' —
'You can wear what you like on your head here,' said the orderly.

High standard of graffiti on the Secure Unit lav wall —
I read:
God does play dice with the Universe —
and She's losing

IN WATERSTONE'S:
'I want a book on the Duke of Edinburgh' —
'Well, there isn't one' —
'Oh' —
'Which is funny – because there *are* rumours —
No. All we've got is these:' —
The Duke – A Portrait of Prince Philip —
'Well that's what I want!' —
'OH! I thought you meant a scandal book! Well, you can
    have *these* —
they're not even worth remaindering now' —
In effect I only had one book —
He'd given me both the paper – and hardback of:
The Duke – A Portrait of Prince Philip by Tim Heald* —

*published by Hodder & Stoughton, 1991.

Apparently, our Royal Family don't have a family tree —
they have a Family Jungle —
so dense no one man could pick his way through —
except maybe the Duke *has* (I was reading on the tube) —
The Duke's a whizz at deck hockey —
likely to take your legs off if you're between him and the ball —
I picked up a bottle of Scotch at the off-licence —
Parked at the end of my road was a Licence Detector Van —
but I allowed myself no paranoia —
after all, it had to be somewhere! —

I was excited by the fact this was a book nobody was reading —
It made it a Gants Hill book —
Bibliomancy! —
I plunged into the middle —
and opened it at page 160 where the Duke's on a train
    with the author —
and he's talking about BILLY CONNOLLY! —
I went to underline it —
Shame to muck up the hardback —
decided to use the paperback to make notes in —
AND BILLY CONNOLLY WASN'T IN IT! —
And it's not a question of space —
there's room for Billy Fucking Connolly there! —
I could think of many innocent explanations for the omission —
But I was possessed only by SINISTER ONES . . .

Index:
Connolly is featured in neither index —
But I'll tell you what is:
'Vanuatu, veneration for Philip, 144' —
I read it —
My God! —
I've got my show —
I'm gonna ring Richard Eyre now —
It was half past two in the morning —
He sounded sleepy —
I thought, This'll rouse him —
I said, 'Richard! I've got it – listen to this! —
This is out of Tim Heald's book: *A Portrait of Prince Philip* —
and it's not a scandal book —
in fact it so *isn't*, they can't sell it:

> 'One missing spot in his tour of the South Pacific was
> Vanuatu, 1500 miles east of Queensland and . . . where
> the Duke of Edinburgh is worshipped independently of the
> Queen . . .
>   'As the shadows of the great banyan tree lengthen and
> flying foxes flicker through the dusk, there is one particular
> [item] to which the Iounahanan give their undivided
> attention . . . the framed photograph of the Duke . . . [which]
> is an object of veneration . . . The photograph shows the Duke
> in jacket and tie, and appears to be personally signed.'

The Licence Detector Van had now moved right outside my
    house —
Who could they be monitoring at a quarter to three in the
    morning?! —
I leaned out of the kitchen, from where I was reading to
    Richard, and fired the remote up the hall into the living
    room —
There was nothing on! —
Except on ITV —
there was a film —

just finishing —
the credits rolling . . .

'These people – the Iounahanan – are . . . "permanently
spaced out on kava", the local root-based hooch which is
very considerably stronger than Scotch . . . The men sit in
their huts . . . staring into space, while the women do all the
work. The women wear grass skirts, and the men nothing but
"nambas", or penis [wrappers]: straw codpieces which hold the
sexual organ in a permanently erect position – the chief . . . has
sent a namba to Buckingham Palace so that the Duke may wear
it on his visit.'

The van was still outside —
The TV screen had gone blank —

'If the Queen accompanies him, she must be careful not to
see him drinking kava, because if she does, the local rules
insist that she be executed summarily and on the spot, with
a single blow on the head with a giant root. If she does not
accompany him, the Duke will be allocated three wives bearing
a dowry of pigs and pillows. If he wants more he may have to
wait, but . . . there will be no problem over this . . .
    '. . . the Duke has never paid them a visit.

'But the thing is, man, the Ice Age is imminent! —
The whole of civilization is going to break down! —
The French are going to blast a whole new continent up
    in the South Pacific —
And the Duke's involved —
I don't know on what side —
probably his own —
And Billy Connolly! —
but he was scared off and mysteriously disappeared from
    the paperback —
Anyway, so I'll get to Vanuatu —
I can see my rim! —
I'm half-way up my dome!!' —

'I've written about you ringing me up late in my book*,'
  said Richard —
'Oh. Why – do I do it a lot?' —
'Yes.' —

I had no memory of ever having done it before —

Jamais vu – ?! —

A gentle voice from the living room:
'That's the end of broadcasting for tonight, Kenneth' —

I was on a plane with a load of chickens —
live chickens in bags of woven leaves —
stacked on the seats —
The chickens (just their heads poking out of the tops of
  the bags) seemed to accept it all —
When some chickens expressed doubt: *Porrrr!* —
others comforted them: *Beeeeeeh!* —

Utopia and Other Places, Bloomsbury, 1993.

We were flying over the stone-age island of Tanna —
Somewhere in the jungle below were the Iounahanan who
    mysteriously worship the Duke of Edinburgh —
We flew over an enormous PIT —
'See the two EYES!' – said the man behind —
'Yasur! The Volcano! Wan bigfala god ia!' —
two exploding furnaces —
The man behind was bringing Holy Sprays into Tanna which
    he hoped to unload onto the 'Rambo Catholic Church' —
Following Independence in 1980, Tanna, one of the islands which
    makes up the Republic of Vanuatu, had mainly reverted from
    Christianity to KASTOM —
and also the John Frum Cargo Cult —
and also worship of Yasur the Volcano —
but the French still run a small Catholic hall whose main
    activity is the showing of Rambo films every Friday —
the tribes who come know the films by heart —
and join in during the showings —
At Easter they lay on a Rambo Passion Play —
It was hoped that the sprays might encourage a return to
    orthodoxy —
'Frank, incense, and myrrh oil. Make the sign of the cross.
    Let us spray' —
PLEN FALDAON! —
the plane had landed in a field —
Plen faldaon just means 'the plane has landed' in the pidjin
    of the islands —
their variant of pidjin is called Bislama —
named after the local sea-slug —
which the Japs use to make their pricks bigger —
and then from somewhere else they get rhinoceros horn to
    give them the required extra energy to use them —
PLEN FALDAON! —
If it'd have crashed, you'd say: PLEN FALDAON
    BAGARUP! —

I'd done three weeks of my one-man shows in Sydney —
Skin-monitoring vans alarm the beaches —
Each morning on the radio they tell you how long you're
      allowed in the sun today:
'Eight minutes . . . fourteen minutes' —
Big on the Hole in the Ozone Myth here —
Sometimes the algal plankton inhibits all watersports —
but the Australians seem happy enough —
probably because they've got their socks sorted —

Explanation:
These socks are from the Sock Shop, Euston Station, England:
they bag out and the elastication leaves a concertina indentation
      on the leg,
and the foot slimes in the shoe within an hour —

These are expensive socks from the classy Kingswear shop
      in Camden town:
'permanently de-odoured heels and toes' they boast —
but the de-odouring impregnation rots away the wool and
      acrylic mix —
These are Newfoundland socks from Newfoundland:
you'd think with their maritime and arctic conditions they'd
      have got their socks sorted:
but the woolly buff is gone after three washes and then
      they dry like cardboard, like dead salt cods —

These green socks from Don's Fishing-Tackle Emporium are
      certainly warm,
hardwearing;

but a footwash and tweezering is required last thing,
to remove green buff and straggle from the nails, etc., giving
   appearance of mossy feet —
off-putting to a partner – (could choke Fergie) —

But the Australians have got their socks sorted:
'The Holeproof Computer Sock': they grip the whole leg;
'They fall up, not down' – (That's because they're Australian
   socks!) —
I've had my computer socks on all day (and yesterday) —
and to my feet it's as if I've just put on fresh socks;
to be sure if you felt them you'd say: 'Well, they're dampish' —
BUT NOT TO MY FEET! —
They're programmed to give the illusion of freshness TO
   THE FEET —
(You buy them in the chemist.)

Anyway, Colin Watkeys* had managed to pull a marvellous
   stunt with some Aid people in Vanuatu —
I had to do two shows there and they put me up for a
   week on Efaté Island —
My hosts were the VATS people —
not that they pay Vat, or tax for that matter —
The Vats are the Vanuatu Amateur Theatre Society and mainly
   Aid people —
Bringing Aid to the South Pacific is a wonderful life —
Young people! Do try and get in on it if you can —

---

*Colin Watkeys is my One Man Show Agent/Manager and Mate. You ring him if you want
me to perform one of these. His number is 0181-670-1232.

British Aid is paid by for us out of our taxes —
and the first part of the money goes on making sure you
    have a terrific house —
to inspire the people you're bringing Aid to —
give 'em a goal in life —
and the next part of the money goes on flying your kids
    back to the UK,
for a number one education —
and back out to you for holidays (they'll have great holidays!) —
And of course quite some dough goes on bribing some Mr
    Big for you to be allowed to bring Aid to Paradise in the
    first place —
and then if there is any money over you might have to
    do a bit of Aid with it —
but basically the job is: *To seem to do more than the French* —
And if you come by any information as to what the wily
    French are up to, you get a little bit of pocket money on the
    side —
Usually the locals don't want your Aid —
I chummed up with a Water Aid man – a chap from
    Chelmsford —
an ex-Essex waterworks man now bringing water to the tribes —
and he was telling me how he'd go to the Bigman Jif (Chief)
    of a tribe, and say:
'Well Jif, we're going to have to bring this heavy plastic
    piping across your land.'
'WHY?' —
'We're bringing water to the tribes' —
'WE DON'T NEED IT' —
'Well you do – you have to go two miles for your water' —
'WE DON'T' —
'Well you do – you have to get your water from down there —
and that's two miles away' —
'WE DON'T. WE SEND THE WOMEN.'

I'd bought *History of the Three Flags* —
*New Hebrides is changeover to the Republic of Vanuatu** —
It's in three languages: English, French and Bislama Pidjin:

> . . . *bifo waetman i kam fainem yumi, olgeta pipel long evri
> aelans oli frenli pipel, mo olgeta bigfala aelans oli gat pipel
> ˙long hem, mo oli kanibels* —
> . . . before the white man came and discovered us, all the
> people in the islands were friendly; all the bigger islands were
> inhabited and the people were cannibals —

In the New Hebrides colonial days the islands had been run
   by the British and French jointly —
with no emphasis on the jointly —
Two official languages —
two sets of laws —
two sets of law enforcers —
two sides of the road on which to drive —
Called officially the Government of Condominium —
it was dubbed the Government of Pandemonium —

The pidjin language had grown up from the grand old slaving
   and blackbirding days —

---

* *History of the Three Flags* by G. K. Kalsakau, the First Minister of Self-Government; printed by
I.P.V. Printers, 1980. The Moto: LONG GOD YUMI STANAP – IN GOD WE STAND – FIDÈLE EN DIEU.

Us and the French had grabbed chaps randomly to work
   plantations —
shovel batshit out of guano caves —
And two thousand different island languages —
The poor buggers couldn't talk to each other —
so they'd adopted the persecutor's tongue —
the English pidjin being preferred to the French —
(the French, even while flogging them, had been prissy about
   pronunciation) —
The French had agreed to allowing Pidjin English to be the
   semi-official native language —
but had insisted on organizing the spelling —
and for humour they made it completely loony —
like *church* is spelled '*jioj*' —

The weekly paper's in the three languages —
On this page I'm mentioned:

> Ken will perform two different plays in Vila . . . blah de
> blah . . . Ken's newest play will be first performed at the
> National Theatre in London, so you will see that he really
> is quite famous.

and here's a joke —

Jokes. Laugh yourself to tears
*Tu olfala, John mo Tom, i live long Ambrym. Tufala ia i
gat bigfala garen. Wan moning, John i talem long Tom se hemi
luk wan flaeng fox i stap kakae wan banana blong Tom . . .*

Problem here with John and Tom, you see, with a flying
   fox eating Tom's bananas —
Island jokes always begin with a flying fox —
the flying fox is rarely a significant part of the joke —
but it alerts us that we may be
   heading into humour —

Man blong 8 Yia long Tudak

Long las wik, yumi ridim se hemi go blong lukaot kokonat crab mo afta we hemi saenem "wan samting", devel o Setan mi no save. Taem toslaet i det, hemi pre mo klaem wan ston afta i stap singsing "My God can do anything". Afta (hemi stap andap long ol stone ia) hemi harem bodi blong hem i narakaen, i sek i foldaon long solwota mo semtaem tu wan weif i kam. "Mi karem toslaet blong mi, mo taem mi kilim weif olsem ia, toslaet blong mi i laet bakegen mo mi no mo save offem"..... **Part II mo Faenol storian blong man blong 8 yia long Tudak, Kalsaupia Herbert.**

Taem hemi kasem bak haos, hemi soem toslaet ia we i laet strong nomo long ol famili blong hem mo ol fren.

Hemi switjim "off" be toslaet ia i no save off. Mekem hemi lego toslaet ia i on nomo istap.

Samting i mekem hem long 1983 long taem ia, humi gat samwei 27 yia.

Taem hemi kasem haos ia, hemi stat blong lanem back-saed blong hem i soa, be nomo hemi no mekem soa blong hem ia i winim hem, molong manis Februari, namba 15 blong sem yia, i go putum sista blong hem long Malapoa College.

Taem hemi stap long Vila, hemi go luk wan man Tongo blong i luk'uk hem be nomo hemi harem se bak blong hem i stap semak nomo.

Wan bigfala boela i kamaot long baksaed blong hem mo boela ia i gat seven tut.

Siknes blong hem mo longtaem we istap insaed i mekem se hemi nomo save talem se long 1983 or 1984 nao hemi go insaed.

(Be folem storian blong mifala, maet Kalsaupia i stap ova long 8 yia ia insaed long tudak from ol last deit mo yia we hemi stap tokbaot hemi ol deit blon gyia 1983.)

Taem bigfala boela ia i mekem hem i mekem se hemi stap longdaon nomo mo hemi stap kolkol. "Mi stap laydown nomo mo mekem se mi stap insaed nomo, afta Mummy nao i stap wetem mi oltaem. Taem mi wantem wan samting, hemi mekem blong mi, kakae, tea, 8 yia ia mi stap insaed", Kalsaupia i talem.

"Mi no sik, siknes ia nomo mi stap kolkol" hemi talem.

Mekem se ino sik be fasin blong stap harem kolkol ia i mekem se hemi stap insaed 8 yia (or bitim).

Taem hemi go insaed ia hemi no moa kamaot, yes i nomo kamaot long doa. Blong 8 yia ia hemi stap insaed nomo.

VATS

Continued from last week.

Ken will perform two different plays in Vila, the first will be at Le Lagon on Wednesday 3rd February and will be a normal theatre evening. The second performance will be at a Gala dinner at Le Lagon on Friday 5th February. Tickets are Vt1500 for the play and Vt4000 for the dinner.

The visit is sponsored by VATS and Le Lagon Hotel. VATS are most grateful to the British High Commission and the British Council for their help in contacting Ken Campbell. It seems that one of Ken's plays is set in an island called Efate, and when he heard that there was an active Theatre Group in Port Vila he was very keen to come and perform his play here. Ken's newest play will be first performed at the National Theatxre in London, so you will see he really is quite famous.

Since it is the policy of VATS to try to bring good theatre to everybody they have kept the prices as low as possible and to see the same show in Sydney would cost at least twice the Vila price, so this will be a wonderful opportunity to see a top professional performing his own plays.

flying foxes being particularly batty-looking —
and nice in a stew apparently —

But this is the big story:

Man blong 8 Yia long Tudak

a man was eight years in the total darkness —

> *Long las wik, yumi ridim se hemi go blong lukaot kokonat crab mo afta we hemi saenem 'wan samting', devel o Setan mi no save.*

Long las wik: last week —
yumi ridim: you and I read —
se hemi go blong lukaot kokonat crab: how this guy went to look
    at a coconut crab —
(they're these enormous land crabs) —
mo afta we hemi saenem 'wan samting': and how this crab
    was signing that he wanted something —
devel o Setan mi no save: whether it was the Devil, or Satan,
    we don't know yet —
Anyway, the guy who got summoned by the coconut crab, was
    a Mr Kalsaupia Herbert and this is the second instalment of
    Mr Herbert's sensational story —
which hinges on this paragraph here:

> *Wan bigfala boela i kamaot long baksaed blong hem mo boela ia i gat seven tut —*

That's to say: *Wan bigfala boela*: one enormous boil —
i kamaot long baksaed blong hem: it came out of his backside —
mo: and more to tell you —
boela ia i gat seven tut: this 'ere boil,
    it HAD SEVEN TEETH! —

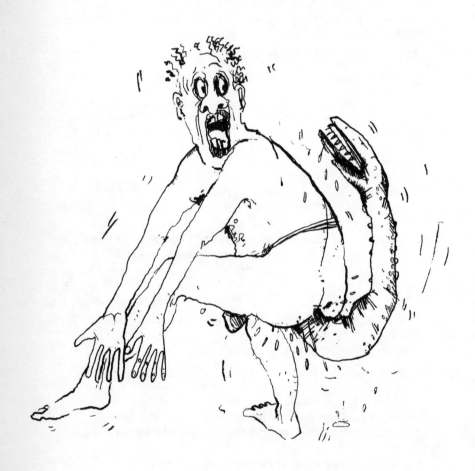

I was pretty clear on this —
there are only about 800 words of pidjin —
and I'd looked it all up in the dictionary:
*Evri samting yu wantem save long Bislama be yu fraet tumas
blong askem** —

I asked my Water Aid friend about Mr Herbert's boil —
I said, 'These seven teeth, what does it mean? —
Was it a sevenbulbed haemorrhoid?' —
'NO,' he said, 'YOU HAVEN'T GOT THE PICTURE AT
   ALL —
IT WASN'T ATTACHED TO HIM —
IT EXPLODED OUT OF HIS ARSE AND WAS SNAPPER-
   ING UP AT HIM!' —
'Gawd,' I said, 'No wonder he spent eight years in the Tudak.'

Anyway, while he was in the Tudak he heard voices —
and some of these voices he heard were singing voices —
and they taught him a whole hymn book of new hymns —
and when, after his eight long years, he was eventually lured
   out of the Tudak —
he married seven women —
one wife for each tooth of the boil —
and he now tours the jungles with his choir of wives,

**Evri Samting . . . Everything you wanted to know about Bislama but were
afraid to ask – A Traveller's Guide to Vanuatu Pidgin English* by
Darrell Tyron. A Media Masters (South Pacific) Pidgin Post Publication.

telling his story and teaching the new hymns —
(this is the sort of news it's worth being addicted to).

'So, what on earth was this boil, then?' I asked my Aid mate —
He said that this sort of thing happened not infrequently
   in these parts —
maybe it was a partially formed parasitic twin,
prompted into anal birth by the French Underground Nuclear
   testing —
Fish now, on occasion, climbed up trees —
turtles came ashore to lay their eggs,
did a weird dance, and then wandered inland to snuff it —
And you must have noticed that the local trousers and shorts
   have lace-up bottoms?
Yes, I had? —
'IT WAS LAST YEAR,' he said —
'WE HAD THIS PLAGUE OF BALD-HEADED MICE —
THAT RUN UP YOUR LEGS AND GUM YOU —
EDIBLE, APPARENTLY —
THE LOCALS LIKE THEM' —
but he'd never fancied it —
'Doesn't it worry you being here?' I asked —
'No, it suits me here,' he said —
Back in Chelmsford his balls had been going mouldy in the
   fluorescent light.
News of Kalsaupia Herbert's boil had broken the same week
   that the Queen gave her 'Annus Horribilis' speech —
And ex-pat wits referred to the Kalsaupia Herbert phenomenon
   as the 'Anus Mirabilis' —

I was asking about where they worship the Duke of Edinburgh —
'O that's not here, you'd have to go to Tanna —
but it's not on the tourist track —
you'd be headed into nambus territory —
Do you know what a nambus is?' —
'Yes, it's a penis wrapper' —
'And it's John Frum country . . .' —

Since the 1900s, Tanna had been mainly in the charge of
    our military-backed Presbyterians —
We gave 'em the option of converting to Christianity —
called 'oli pulim trousis': everyone get your pants on —
or having your village shelled —
and the Tannese saw the light in quite some number —
and when you converted, your land was then held 'in trust'
    by the church —
but if you reverted: 'oli lusim trousis' —
you didn't get it back —
And our Presbyterians had braved the jungle and disease —
(twenty years it took them) —
to locate all Tanna's magic rocks and stones —
and they'd dug them all up —
and tossed them in the sea —
at Green Point —
they'd banned the drinking of *kava* —
a non-alcoholic but heavily narcotic root-based drink —
they'd banned singing and dancing and the recital of myths —
they'd banned eating each other and the swapping of wives —
and they'd banned the wearing of the nambus* —
and the Hundred-Day Circumcision Ritual —

*'The penis wrapping displays rather than conceals – a much stronger effect of
indecency than nakedness' – The Presbyterian Missionary Society.

This is really a SURcision or SUPERcision business —
When they're eight or so, the young lads present their plonkers
     to the Rock —
and Wap! the flint axe comes down —
and they're led off into the jungle —
they're not going to see their mums now for a hundred days —
and odds and sods and bits and pieces are entered into the
     wound —
all according to ancient *kastom* practice —
(and the kids mustn't touch themselves for the whole one
     hundred days —
they have to eat with their elbows) —
but it means that each lad winds up with an individualized,
     *kastom*ized donger worth the having —
and the lads are of course subjected to a variety of indignities
     during this time —
To help them become men —
the elders of the village paint faces on their arses and prance
     in at them backwards —
and shit on their heads —
The enforced homosexuality will of course come to an end
     at the end of the hundred days —
unless some lad shows some special calling in this area —
Similar to our Scouts —
the Scout Movement was from its inception a device for
     supplying pederasts with a vast choice of lads —
the founder even calling his book *Scouting for Boys*! —
They're basically vegetarians out there —
but at the end of the hundred days, they bonk a load of
     pigs with ceremonial pig bonkers —
which is something of a sacrifice:
a pig is regarded as one quarter human there —
and they're cocky little chaps, their pigs —
I'd go along with that —
A woman who's suckling will be expected to suckle the runt
     of a pig litter —

(which is apparently quite a caper —
and much loved by the ladies —
one of the great joys of motherhood) —
And they become 'family pigs'.

Do you know, there are no cases of post-natal depression there?
I pass these things on . . .

Anyway, they bonk some pigs —
and the kids are reunited with their mums —
and then watch as their mums rape the village geezers —
in bunches of three or more, the mums pounce —
one sitting on your head —
another roaring your kastomized manhood to the skies —
and Yasur! —

Anyway, all these joys had been denied the Tannese by the
   Presbyterians —
Then in 1937 had ariz the Messiah! —
JOHN FRUM HE COME —
Out of the sea at Green Point, Tanna —
a white man of military bearing in a bowler hat had stepped
   FROM THE SEA —
and he gave his name as John Frum —

Jake Kratis he no come —
John Frum he come

goes the triumphant hymn —
Jesus Christ, or Jake Kratis as they call him there,
has been promising a return visit for 2000 years —
but so far no show —
and *there's the difference* —
JOHN FRUM HE COME —
a white man, yes, but his white body sheathing a black soul —
a spirit of the Tannese ancestors —
and more than twenty-eight indigenous languages on Tanna —
but John Frum, he spoke every man his own tongue —
And his first commandment was: 'LUSIM BIBEL!' —
Sling all your Bibles into the sea, boys! —
We want the singing back and the dancing back! —
and we want the KAVA back! —
and we'll swap our wives —
and strap on the nambus! —
and we want the Grand Old Hundred Days back! —
Plus one for me! —

And the hunt was on —
This was an uprising —
and that's when the descriptions of John Frum change —
one day he's thin —
one day he's fat —
he's tall —
he's short —
and then he's not white, he's a blackfala whited up —
and he's caught many times —
but it's never HIM —
And planty blackfala rounded up and questioned —
some shot —
or sent off to do time jail Efaté —
and the Good News of John Frum, him spread to other islands —

and John Frum he comes to our boys in Efaté jail each
   night at six —
'HE COME IN THE WALLS' —
'What do you mean? He could walk through the walls?' —
'NO – HE COME IN THE WALLS —
HE TEACH OUR BOYS KNOCKKNOCK TALK!' —
'What – Morse you mean?' —
'Yes' —

And he said his legions of five thousand strong were down
   Yasur the Volcano —
and he said that one day Yasur would roar up and join
   all the islands together —
And maybe that's where the French got their fiendish plan from! —
And the Church of John Frum has a red cross —
But it's nothing to do with crucifixions —
IT'S TO EXCITE FOOD PARCELS YOUR WAY! —

John Frum said: 'Don't work too hard —
And I will be with you at KAVA time' —

I went to the little Efaté tourist office —
'Can you get me to Tanna?' —
'Yes, but you'll have to go on the chicken run' —
As to visiting the tribes who worship the Duke of
   Edinburgh, they said there's no way they could
   arrange that! —
Best thing, they said, was to book on all
   the tours —

'When your guide sees all your vouchers —
every voucher represents a little bit for them you see —
maybe they'll be so happy they'll see what they can do for you' —
It isn't half expensive, the jungle —
All my profits three weeks Sydney going on two days Tanna —

For real jungle use, you need what they call the Mae Vest —
with its pockets like sacks —
On one side of my Mae Vest, I'd stuffed my sink plunger,
    dicknose, laughing mirror, my comedy teeth, shaving soap
    and false arm —
I was to be staying with Jif Tom Numake, the paramount
    jif of the island —
Maybe Jif Tom Numake would want to hear some of my stories —
I wasn't going to be pushy —
but I wanted to be ready —
On the other side of my Vest, I was stocked with Spam —
I'd asked Chelmsford if he'd got any tips . . .
He said:
One: Pose as an American —
They're not keen on Brits (or French) —
but they like Americans —
When the Americans landed in the War,
they learned the natives' names —
No whiteman had ever done that before —
they put up cinema tents and let them come in and watch
    the films —
and taught them 'Way down upon the Swanee River' —
Two: Take Spam —
Spam!? —
Yeah. If you're going after the Iounahanan —
you maybe want to be crossing some tribe's territory —
'Can I go across here?' you say —

'Sure,' they say, 'HAVE YOU GOT ANY SPAM?'

Theroux* talks about the Spam obsession conundrum of the
    South Pacific —
Quite frankly, he says, I think it's because it's the nearest
    thing to people —
When Theroux was on Tanna, he asked Jif Tom if, since
    Independence, people are again being eaten on Tanna —
O, says Jif Tom, I dunno, I mean, well . . .

Even empty Spam tins have value —
Inspector comes round:
'Anything been going on here?' . . .
'No . . .
er . . . we had some Spam the other night . . .' —
OLI FRENLI PIPEL, MO OLI KANIBELS —
South Pacific cannibalism should not be confused with that
    awful American sordid serial people-eating —
(Jeffrey Dahmer was found SANE —
because he always put on a condom before he fucked the
    corpses before he ate them —
I just thought you'd like to know the current American legal
    definition of sanity —
if we're going to get into anthropological comparison) —

*Paul Theroux, *The Happy Isles of Oceania – Paddling the Pacific*, Penguin 1993.

There's always been a lack of protein on these islands —
Okay for fruit and veg – but for protein they've really just
   got their pigs —
which they prefer to save for times of celebration,
like the toughening up of little lads' knobs —
If *you'd* only got a nambus, wouldn't you prefer that your
   valuable protein went to your family, your tribe? —
Barbaric no? – to bury your valuable stuff for the benefit
   of worms? —
But we've taught them a better way now —
and they're adequately supplied with Spam and soya chunks —
in return for their timber and mineral rights.

PLEN FALDAON! —
The airport is a shed (no glass in the window) at the edge
   of a field —
and my Sprayman is met and whisked off to the Rambo
   Catholic Church —
The chickens are united with their new owners —
But there's no one to meet me —

I'd been told that a representative of Jif Tom would meet me —
but there is no one to meet me —
and the plane is now taking off —
and there's no one for me . . .

There are people there – quite a lot – who seem to have
  some 'airfield existence' —
but none look at me —
as if I'm invisible —
'Garlands of flowers, singing and dancing, and the recital
  of myths, tales and poetry' —
is what the *Encyclopædia Britannica** says of the culture of
  the South Pacific —
Well, it seems it's gone —
thrown into the sea with the magic stones —

I feel my Spam —
The Spam gives me courage —
Chap with back to me —
a back of ritual nobbles —
'Hello . . .' (friendly) —
'Britis?' (unfriendly) —
'No, American – Spam, chum?' —
I gave him a tin —
But he'd seen the loaded pocket of my Mae Vest —
he wanders away to some friends —
showing them the Spam —
mumbling —
Shit! – they're gonna rush me —
(you get murdered for less in Florida and Finsbury Park) —
Ladies are looking at me now —
they're probably rampant mums —
Cotton wool! —
(My comedy teeth are wrapped in cotton wool) —
I stuff some of the cotton wool in my ear —

* *Encyclopædia Britannica* available from airports,
some stations, and selected Texas Home Care stores.

Looking in at me through the glassless window frame of
   the airport shed:
JOHN BIRT —
calm —
and then he started to fade —
But I could still see his outline —
and it had imprinted on the retina —
wherever I blinked I saw Birt's outline —
his glasses —
like a John Birt logo —

Whatever the explanation —
it was . . . COMFORTING.

And then she arrived —
my guide Pauline —
a local lady – and I loved her —
You can use this fuzzy hair for keeping things in, you know —
like pencils, rulers, notebook —
Pauline asked if I had any tour vouchers —
I showed her my full set —
She looked made up! —
I asked about the Duke of Edinburgh —
she'd never heard of him —
'There's a tribe who worship him —
he's their god —

the Duke of Edinburgh —
Philip . . .'
'PILIP!' —
'Yeah! Pilip!' —
Apparently there were two tribes still worshipping PILIP —
Jif Tuk's tribe —
and Jif Jack Naiva's —
Could I meet them? —
'I don't know . . .' —
'I gat Spam,' I said, flowing open the pocket of my Mae
    Vest —
'We see' —

Maybe we'd pick up some news in the John Frum Cargo
    Cult Church —
half an hour away in the jeep —
and it's woven —
a woven church —
And a gaunt old priestess, who told me all about everything
    with her mouth closed —
(John Frum had appeared to her in a dream —
and taught her the secret of international speak —
which is: Keep your mouth closed —
John Frum he say, 'It's only when you open your mouth
    to speak that confusion occurs') —
Pauline was asking her about the possibility of visiting Pilip
    tribes . . .
Priestess emitted hopeful hum —
And they went off in the jeep together —
leaving me alone in the woven church of John Frum —
I wandered to a woven bookshelf —
Sign:
DON'T NICKEM THE BUKS —

I pulled out *Did the Virgin Mary Live and Die in England?**
by Victor Dunstan —
O, could I have travelled back thirty years and gone into
the Gants Hill Library with this one! —
It has it all!:
Jesus, Mary, and Joseph the Carpenter, yeah, yeah —
but those of us who went to Sunday School know there's
another Joseph:
Joseph of Arimathea —
but we never quite got to grips with who he was —
Well, he's Virgin Mary's uncle —
and he was a tin man —
I don't mean like in the *Wizard of Oz*! —
he was importing tin into the Holy Land —
and he was getting most of it from CORNWALL —
and you remember the Slaughter of the Innocent,
and King Herod getting in a tiz and wiping out all the young
babes and kids? —
Well Uncle Joseph said,
'Come on Virgin, get on one of my boats – you and babe
Jesus – and go to Cornwall' —
Now I'd always thought we were berking about in blue and
woad until the Romans came and sorted out the plumbing —
But not at all! —
Cornwall was where the Celts were, and the Druid gentlemen —
Cornwall was the envy of the civilized world! —
Let's get you there Virgin —
and yea! she did come —
with the infant Jesus —
(the Carpenter didn't come we don't think) —
She was a Virgin as you know when she had Jesus —
But she made up for it in Cornwall —
had loads more kids —
by several Cornish fathers —

*Megiddo Press Ltd, Grosvenor House, 20 St Andrews Crescent, Cardiff, South Wales.

They were happy there —
but when He was thirty-nine —
(this thirty-three business is a nonsense, says Dunstan —
and listen, he's an accountant – so he's done his arithmetic
    on this) —
Jesus got fixed on the idea of going back to the land of his birth,
and telling all the Rabbis and Pharisees and everyone all
    about Celt and Druid culture —
And people said He was daft —
but there was no stopping Him —
And He did go, with the unfortunate result you've no doubt
    read about —
But Mary came back – she really loved it here —
and she's buried at Glastonbury —
But Jesus had some French children —
(a holiday he went on) —
whose descendants are the French kings Merovech and
    Dagobert —
whose Royal HOLY LINE enters our Royal Family through
    Henry VI and Henry VIII,
winding up with our Queen AND Prince Philip —
the both of them being direct descendants of Queen Victoria —
(but not *first* cousins —
so their kids shouldn't be potty) —
and Joseph of Arimathea's Cornish line goes like this:
Joseph of Arimathea's daughter Anna's daughter Penardin
    married King Lear —
so Virgin Mary's uncle is Goneril's great-grandfather —
a fact I was unaware of . . .

I heard the return of Pauline's jeep —
the news was good:
Jif Jack Naiva would be pleased to grant me an
    audience.

Less than half an hour's drive —
and a hut of weave —
Painted on its outside in big letters:
JOHN FRUM —
and a square wooden sign —
fading but legible —
in perfect English:

**WE BELIEVE PRINCE PILIP
IS ORIGINALLY OF TANNA
AND WE WANT HIM TO RETURN HOME**

Pauline was in the hut —
she called for me to come in —
and there was this fine old man —
wearing nothing but his nambus —
a long business, past his knees —
of straw I think —
like a horse's tail, like a witch's broom* —
And on a woven-topped table:
a signed photo of Pilip —
and a mouldering coffee-table Coronation book —
and the centrepiece a biscuit tin, with the Queen on one
  side and his Duke god on the other —
I have never handled any religious item with as much reverence
  as Jif Jack's Biscuit Tin —
And ready for the Duke, a rush-matting bed —
and laid out for him, a crisp new nambus —
(which is worn 'bollocks out') —

---

*Tim Heald's book is in error in his nambus description. The Tannese nambus has never held
'the sexual organ in a permanently erect position'. He is muddling it with the nambus styles
of Erromango and Malekula.

I said to Pauline: 'I'm not sure he'll find it all that
　　comfortable at first' —
She said: 'I'm sure in his case he can make it nice for
　　himself with a hanky' —

'Has he actually met Pilip?' —
'Yes' —
'And he said he'd be coming back?' —
'Yes' —
Jif Jack had a question for me – which he conveyed to
　　me through Pauline —
The Jif wants to know if it's true that Pilip has a black knob —
This was clearly a devotional rather than flippant enquiry —
I said: 'Yes, as far as I know he has, although I haven't
　　actually seen it' —
The religion of Pilip-worship is called Pilipanity —
or Pilipanty —
and the creed of it seems to be roughly this:
Pilip is a Tannese soul —
a Spirit of the Ancestors —
but currently trapped in a white body —
but a white body of some significance —
a white body that can be traced back to Jake Kratis – (see
　　Dunstan) —
Pilip is not God Almighty —
and not to be compared with Yasur the Volcano god —
or even John Frum —
but a handy little household god —
a flawed god —
tendency to flirtiness and arrogance —
and currently undergoing punishment —
which is why he is under the thumb of the
　　grumpy woman you can see on the front of
　　British banknotes —

His secret goal is to pump the hot holy blood back into
   the black tribes —
and especially into Tanna, because Tanna is the centre of
   the world,
and also that's where his great spirit originally hails from —
Jif Jack keeps three virgins always ready for the Duke —
and pigs —
and pillows —
and they've been ready for him for nearly thirty years —
(fresh virgins every two years or so) —
When I got back to London I rang up a retired High
   Commissioner for the islands —
'Did the Duke ever go there?' I asked him —
'No. Absolutely not, old boy' —
'Well Chief Jack thinks he did' —
'I'm sure he does think he did and I expect he's convinced,
but you know they make no difference between dream and
   reality in their culture?'
'Mmm' —
'And do you know the strength of that stuff they drink?' —

All I read these days are books about the South Pacific —
I plough through old missionary books —
and any new stuff that comes out —
This is a nice little book:
Coconuts and Coral by Gwendoline Page* —
what life was like on the islands years ago, from a British
   housewife's point of view —
And on page 37 there is a photograph of:

   The British and French Commandants of Police meeting
   HRH the Duke of Edinburgh on his visit to the New

*Printed and published 1993 by Geo. R. Reeve Ltd, Damgate, Wymondham, Norfolk.

Hebrides in March 1971. The Duke is escorted by the
Resident Commissioner Mr M. Townsend. On the right
of the picture is District Agent Dick Hutchinson

The Duke is in white Admiral of the Fleet kit with medals
    and sword —
and on page 196, Mrs Page details the native dances which
    were danced for him on this occasion —
So I think he went to the islands, m'lud —
YES, BUT HE NEVER WENT TO TANNA! —
so he didn't go to the only island that remembers him —
the only island that yearns for his RETURN.
We can only suggest he goes on less visits —
and maybe he'd be worshipped in more places . . .

Anyway, they take the idea of his Return very seriously
    on Tanna —
and they've woven a palace for him —
in a banyan tree —
and from there, he and Jif Tuk and Jif Jack Naiva will
    rule the world —

A British newspaper cutting on Jack's table:

PHILIP'S KICK IN THE GOULASH

Jif Jack pointed me towards it with concern —
and I don't think he was worried about rudeness to Hungarians —
I think he was worried about how old the Duke looks now —
that time is running out —
by the time he got there he wouldn't be up to his Holy Task —
(unless he was the Great Spunko —
but as Jake says: 'It's a bit tasteless from a wheelchair') —

But why??
How??

I put it together this way:
In the run-up to Independence there was fear that there
    would be no British influence left on the Island of Tanna —
the Presbyterians had made us too unpopular —
they couldn't wait for us to go —
the charmingness of the phrase OLI PULIM TROUSIS conceals
    a scar —
THE POISON WAS IN THE TROUSIS! —
BUSINESS INTERESTS HAD SEEN THEIR CHANCE! —
We supplied 'em with diseased trousis —
they had measles etc. in 'em —
and we got the population down from 20,000 to 6,000 —
thus liberating valuable land for the intensive growing of
    coconuts —
COCONUTS!? —
for the copra —
WHAT IS COPRA? —
It's dried coconut flesh and it's used in the making of SOAP —
'Lever's Easy-Shaving Stick'! —

Bong! —
I said to Pauline, 'Me and my dad have used that soap' —
'How could you do that?' —
'Well, they didn't actually stress this aspect in their advertising' —

So a British High Commissioner, who knew the thinking of
    the island,
had steamed over there with some crap from the Coronation,
and some dangerous Gants Hill books,
and got Pilip accepted as some half-arsed John Frum —
So we've still got a fingerhold of influence there —
and the French too, with their Rambo Catholic Church.

Pauline said, 'Jif Jack would like you to take kava with him' —
'That would be an honour' —
'You must realize, I cannot come with you' —
'Yes, of course – Is there anything I should know?' —
'It would be better if you wore less closis —
You see how far Jif Jack stands from you? —
It's not because he doesn't like you – he has fright of your closis.'

Pauline went back to the jeep —
in fact she went off in the jeep —
Jif Jack chatted on for a few minutes with his mouth shut —
and then nodded and left – presumably to round up the
    other Pilipanties for the kava-drinking ceremony.

I was alone now in the hut . . .
'Wear less closis' . . .
I took off my shirt and hoped that'd do —
Then it occurred to me that I had the chance of a lifetime here —
to take a picture of myself in the Duke's nambus for the
    NT programme —
poster even —
I stripped right down —
I'd come to Tanna without a handkerchief . . .
so I 'made it nice for myself' with a computer sock —
and then I thought, *Let's really go for it!* —
So I put my comedy Doddy teeth in —
rammed on the sink plunger . . .

and Jif Jack came in with eight Pilipanties —
You think like lightning at times like these:
I whipped the Royal Nambus off and back on the bedmat —
and I quickly whisked out the Doddy teeth —
but I dropped them! —

and . . .
the Pilipanty party stood transfixed —
BY THE TEETH —
they were scooped up with reverence on a Royal postcard —
and then I realized:
THEY THOUGHT THEY'D DROPPED OUT OF MY ARSE!
and that I was therefore some jungle prophet in the Kalsaupia
   Herbert mode —
and hitching up my sock, I followed my hosts to the kava grove.

The Kava Ceremony was to take place beneath Pilip's banyan
    tree palace —
John Frum hymns first – 'Sing sing long John Frum' —
and then they look to me —
it is assumed that if I have the gift of anal dentures I also
    compose hymns —
I gave them:

'Onward Christian soldiers, onward Buddhist priests —
Onward fruits of Islam, fight till you're deceased —
Fight in richest battle, with arum-pah-poom —
For the greater glory o-of Pilip and John Frum —
Ra ra ra ra ra ra —
HOY!' —

Hoy! rather than *phthhhbpt!* —
phthhhbpt! was too gross for this gentle assembly —
(Actually I learned later that to go *phthhhbpt!*
    at a Kava Ceremony is an execution offence —
You get brained on the spot with a giant root —
so I was quite lucky there) —
'Don't work too hard
and I will be with you at kava time' —

Kava: The spindly roots of Piper methysticum —
scraped, peeled, and chewed to pulp by uncircumcised male
    virgins —
and the results of their labours (like dog sick the second
    time round)
spat on leaves, then transferred onto a square of matting,
and a small amount of water poured on it and patted into it,
and pushed through into an enamel potty —
Tanna kava: The strongest – they say – in the whole South
    Pacific —

and it's drunk in silence —
If you wish to say anything, you must make your words
    no more than the breeze in the banyan tree —
The form is to listen to the advice of the Ancestors in the
    rustle of the leaves —
OOO-WISH —
the wind through the sacred banyan tree —
It's in the banyan tree they stick the skulls —
The Tannese recipe for people is: well-done with bread fruit —

There was much silent ruminative examination of my Doddy
    dentures —
I put them in for them —
There was no hilarity —
they were marvelled at —
they were no more comic than a feather in the nose —
Everyone tried them (they are made to fit ME) —
One man they fitted pretty well . . .

OOO-WISH —
I agreed to a second shell of kava —
It tastes like soil and snot, and the trick is to vault it quick
    past any tastebuds —
Two shells of kava achieves complete jamais vu of both legs,
and my thoughts wandered to the Royal Family,
and wasn't I meant to be saving them? —
or to save the MONARCHY —
OO-WISH —
Hoo-brish?! —
HUBRIS! – ? —

KOROS: HUBRIS: NEMESIS: ATÉ —
The Ancient Greek concept which I'd years ago dismissed
   as unlikely to have any application in the Modern World —
We're the children of Marx —
We're the kids of Freud —
We do things 'cos of our environment —
'cos of seeing our dad's donger at an unsuitable moment —
we haven't the scope for Tragic Choice and Fatal Flaw that
   they had in Ancient Greece —
But how did it go?
Koros: too much —
Hubris: much too much! a resulting arrogance —
but 'arrogance' not really the word for it —
it's a cast of mind which supposes that
THE USUAL RULES DON'T APPLY TO YOU —
YOU ARE SPECIAL AND OKAY —
Nemesis: fate —
Até: destruction —
One of the big numbers of hubris: MASQUERADING AS
   A DEITY! —
at that moment, it's not fair! —
the gods come shrieking out of the skies and wreak havoc
for GENERATIONS TO COME EVERLASTING! —
And wasn't the Duke (one understands, out of duty to Great
   British Business) guilty of masquerading as a deity here? —
so, was down to him all this Squidgy/Prince of Wales coming
   back as an everlastingly unflushable Tampax/Rottweiler
   nonsense —
this reduction of our Royal Family to soap? —
and worse —
to something of less dignity than a busker's routine —
and the Duke responsible for this now endless plague on
   the House of Windsor? —
If so, the chat about some tax from the Queen sometime
   wasn't likely to do ANYTHING! —
The Royal Stable has bolted —

They'd have to give the *lot* away —
Public self-chastisement on the steps of St Paul's —
and even then I was doubtful —

I accepted a third shell of kava —
(the dicknose and laughing mirror were a hit) —
AN ICON! —
only an ICON could save them now:
The Duke comes back – as he's promised —
DUKE WITH JACK . . . (not enough) —
DUKE WASHING JACK'S FEET – JACK PROTESTING
    HIS UNWORTHINESS —
and that becomes The Image —
THE PICTURE – THE ICON! —
Sold in Boots —
outsells Trechiakoff's *Green Lady* —
Should the Duke be in Admiral of the Fleet kit, or nambus,
    as he performs the ablution? —
Is he in computer sock? —
WHOO-HOO-BRISH —
WHOO!
and a fine upsurge of lava from Yasur the God Volcano —
and then I knew that however BRIGHT and SEARING that
    ICON —
that *it wouldn't be enough* —
I could see Yasur —
to halt the plague, the Duke'd have to heave himself into
    Yasur, the core of the world —

Some boys had been summoned to
    perform a Pig Dance for me —

a lot of snuffling and oinking and running around on all fours —
I waited for the end of the entertainment, nodded, and handed
   out some Spam —
then rising onto absent legs —
with a mix of faith, balance and gravity,
I jerked off [? – Ed.] towards the Volcano —
the kava company made no motion to stop me —
in fact they made no motion at all —
most I think may have missed the Pig Dance —
and in fact it may not have happened —
My notion: to research my Tragic Hero to the end of the line —
How does it feel, Pilip, on your final trip to Nemesis? —
Eyes sometimes in the forest —
'John Frum he come,' I said definitely, sometimes adding:
'Mo Pilip' —

On a thorny bush I snagged my sock and had to go back for it —
I had the feeling I was being followed —
But I had no fear —
I was researching the Duke —
Usual rules didn't apply to me —

Up now towards the red rim of Yasur the Volcano, in my
   sock —
I saw it was Jif Jack who was following me, his long
   stylish nambus swinging in the moonlight —
A pig was following him —
'Pilip,' I heard Jack say —
THE THROB OF THE VOLCANO UNDERFOOT —
This thought:

What if Pilip, behind the scenes, is headhunting? —
with his Outward Bound Duke of Edinburgh Award Scheme
    Things,
is secretly amassing the mental and physical cream of the world —
to whip the cadres of the IAE?
WOW!

A LOAD OF EVIL SMELLING SHIT AND ASH —
The Duke wrestling on behalf of all that's good,
in the icy teeth of encroaching chaos —
And I thought of my daughter back in England —
Daisy —
nearly fifteen now – and what for her future? —
To be downloaded? Mechanized? Mutated? Improved? —
NO! —
Outward Bound and join the Duke! —
and I saw Daisy up there with the Duke handling a coach
    and four! —
'Fuck! – Mush! – Fuck!':
Bark it out! —
Dog sledge racing from Anchorage to wherever —
sledging down the encroaching ice caps —
to —
Who? – What? —
TO DO BATTLE! —
You're the HORDES, DAISY! —
And here's **THE ICON**:
PILIP! – WARRIOR GOD KING —
leading his worldwide Outward Bound teams —
(and tribes of half-caste progeny) —
down from the ICY HEIGHTS —
to slice the boxes off the heads of Birt, Katz,
    and the LUVVIE PERIL! —

Looking down now into the Volcano, and it's not like you
    expect —
it's so wide you can't see the other side —
and a mile deep —
and grumbling —
popping —
wheezing —
and then like a cannon blasting hot ash and crap in your face —
and it's shot this stuff up a MILE! —
from literally the bowels of the Earth —
this is SOME FARTING —
I was near enough to the very edge to look right in – there's
    no railing —
(Jif Jack well back, waiting, patiently watching) —
Yasur's two burning EYES —
EYES OF FIRE —
the gouged eyeholes of Oedipus —
Yes Jack, Yasur wan bigfala god! —
'John Frum plantyfala ia!' I said, gesturing down into the
    smelly belching,
and referring to John Frum's legendary army —
'John Frum,' said Jack —
and in that moment . . . I converted to two of Jack's gods:
Yasur and Frum —
'John Frum he come,' I said, 'sing sing long John Frum' —
and then I'd made it to his THIRD:
I HAD THE DUKE IN PINK LIGHT —
PILIP – YASUR – JOHN FRUM – Yeah! —
(I became a believer – I believed in Everything —
I BELIEVED IN BELIEF!) —
The New Trinity —
If only I could grab this moment and bring it home with me —

I could see the potent regenerating power this might have
   in Britain:
JOHN FRUM come to champion the HOMELESS; the New
   Age Traveller Convoys, and all Shirkers of Integrity —
'Don't work too hard and I will be with you at Opening Time' —
The barrister in his box would be a bishop —
YASUR – the mile-wide mouth with the burning eyes
INTO WHICH WE PITCH ALL UNBELIEVERS —
And Pilip —
For Pilip, back home, to enjoy his Grand Mythical Status
   he would have to be RITUALLY SLAIN . . .
AND EATEN! —

But the vision fragmented, revealing another:
Pilip cooked – well-done with bread fruit —
handed round —
but no one really wanting any —
the portions left —
to go off . . . —
No! —
He's alright! —
Pilip's alright —
He's round the back! —
This is a Spam Pilip we prepared earlier —
and we can lay on a Resurrection! —
Yeah! —

I'd seen the Truth but in the same instant corrupted it —

The Duke was guilty of no hubris —
The hubris was mine:
The arrogance of apportioning hubris —
that was my offence —
'Excuse me,' I said . . .
(a smell of smouldering wool —
a spark from the Volcano had set light to my sock) —
'Excuse me,' I said to Jif Jack. And his Pig too was
    taking an intelligent interest:
'. . . there's something I must do – ' —
! —
and clouds of disturbed volcanic ash following my express trip
    down to some sort of answer in the Earth's angry bowels and
    my whole life was flashing before me:
the brown breast suckling me —
the grass, the forest, and learning to come when I was bonged —
THE ACORNS —
! —
Just a minute —
THIS ISN'T MY LIFE! —
I'M SHRIEKING DOWN TO THE CORE OF A VOLCANO,
AND I'VE GOT THE WRONG LIFE FLASHING IN FRONT
    OF ME! —
? —
and it wasn't me —
it was the Pig —
Jif Jack had waited his moment —
and then acted —
sacrificed a family Pig —
probably suckled by a grandchild —
a quarter Human —
For what? —
an *eighth* Human . . .
'Thank iu tumas,' I said:
'Yasur – John Frum – Pilip.'

And Lo! a mighty **BUM** appeared in the sky, and from its
celestial bowels eructated a monstrous BOIL whose dentures
held a SCROLL:

MAKE ALL ONE MIGHTY DUNCIAD —
How drown'd is SENSE and SHAME and RIGHT and
WRONG —
Dee-dah dee-dah dee-dah dee-dah dee BONG!
And Daftnesse spreading Goo and Silly-puttied might,
ART after ART goes out and all's NEWSNIGHT;
And viewers willy-nilly, yea or nay,
Are flickered silly by the Cathars' Ray:
Thy Hand (Great Anarch) lets the Curtain fall
And Universal SILLINESSE buries all.

and *phthhhbpt*! it was gone.

I found the manifestation profoundly depressing —
I absolutely doubted its claim to be from some Godhead —
it was psychotronical intercranial babble —
My oculo-endocrine system was wide open to any arse who
    wanted to access it —
they'd monitored me to here —
Well then, there was no place to go —
Were any of my thoughts now my own? —
HAD THEY EVER BEEN? —
. . . 'Go with the flow . . .' —

In the moonlight, the volcanic ash had the appearance of
 SNOW —
Jif Jack was cold —
He was humming —
And I thought, Well, if they're so keen to recruit me, the
 IAE, and the call comes —
and we of the Élite gather in the National Fortress —
John Birt (in Armani flakjacket): 'Glad you've made it Ken' —
'I'm surprised you wanted me, John' —
'It's Noah's Ark time now, Kenneth —
and we're trying to collect an example of everything we can —
and you're some sort of example of something' —
Old faces . . .
Billy Connolly, Richard Eyre —
Outside in the fifteen-foot snowdrifts, those only part-deranged
 by the previous night's BF overload riot with inane grins —
'The mad are dancing with the mad out there,' says John
 Birt, grimly, and giving the deranged a blast from the NT
 water cannon —
And then we're lifted out by helicopter —
onto a private jet —
and it's years later —
and I'm sitting out with Katz and Birt and the Luvvies —
the Élite —
in Rhône-irrigated Algeria —
or watching the Waters of the Amazon cascade down an
 Iraqi hill —
(after a hard day regulating the pork machine) —
They'll no doubt enjoy my few stories of the South Pacific
 Islands —
before they became a French Continent —
('Garlands of flowers, singing and dancing,
and the recital of Myths, Tales and Poetry') —
and I heard the beat of the Tam Tams calling in the pigs:
BOP BOP bopbop BOP BOP —
and I thought, Prince Pilip, Sir, Your Highness:

you gotta come say hello again disfala —
It's all probably too late for an ICON to be any use —
just come and see him —
we don't have to know! —
it'd round off this curious Inter-Glacial nicely —
But I think a bit of deck hockey with the Virgins is called for —
if it's going to make up in some way for us having used
   them as something to wash with —
BOP BOP bopbop BOP BOP —
— — ● ● — —
MIM! —
And I experienced Toujours Vu with you, Jif Jack, on Mount
   Yasur —
toujours vu —
the moment that won't go away —
a moment before which you couldn't have died —
because you were always here —
and always will be —
long past your days —
And as we walked back down from the Volcano —
one Pig less —
I saw a FLYING FOX —
! —
There's a joke to go, Jack! —
Keep the FAITH, Jack —
Your FAITH must triumph —
. . . Pilip is biding his time —
He'll come —
He'll come in the nick of! —
JUST AS THE FRENCH ARE ROARING UP THEIR NEW
   CONTINENT! —
And Pilip'll nick it off 'em! —
And he'll tell the French to Go Forth and Multiply —
(but in salty Royal Vernacular!) —
PILIP! —
GOD and EMPEROR of the SOUTH PACIFIC.

(And before you go God —
Save the Queen.)

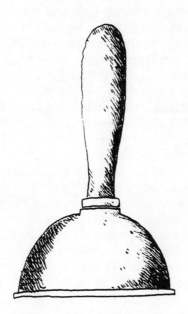

Postscript

From the obituary of Chief Tuk, *Independent*, 2 February 1994, by Nigel Evans

CHIEF TUK was, with Chief Jack Naiva, co-founder of the 'Duke of Edinburgh Cult' on the South Pacific Island of Tanna.

The Duke of Edinburgh Cult and the Jon Frum Cult are the two remaining cargo cults of Melanesia and both unique to Tanna. In fact one grew out of the other.

Portraits of the Royal Family were liberally distributed around the island, and in particular a portrait of Prince Philip holding a revered Tannese chief's baton.*

When I first met Tuk five years ago his little church was already full of gifts from visitors. He was especially delighted with my gift – a small model of Buckingham Palace. I returned a couple of years later to make a film about Tanna for BBC *Everyman*, in which Tuk's fantastic flights of imagination stole the show.

However my own efforts to portray the extraordinary world of the Tannese were eclipsed by the brilliance of a more recent visitor to the island. Ken Campbell based much of his recent one-man show *Jamais Vu* around the Duke of Edinburgh cult. I am sure Tuk would have been quite delighted by it.

---

*Actually a pig bonker. It was sent to Buckingham Palace from Tanna and Prince Philip had himself photographed in a hundred different poses in the hope that one of them would be the right way to hold it. A local pig-bonking expert chose this one for distribution. [Ken Campbell]